Praise for *The Diz*

'A brave and vital anthology by son
voice.

Rae Earl

'A vital anthology with too many constellations of brilliant poets
and poems to pick out individuals; these are important poems of
witness, to one's own body and mind, to institutions, to society
which is failing those who need it most. Ultimately, there is a hope
here, whatever the body has endured, whatever the mind has seen,
there is still poetry where things might be reported or made sense
of, or redeemed.'

Andrew McMillan

'Packed full of the greatest poetic minds you could ever wish to
read, in a moment of need. Anything with Byron Vincent AND
Lemn Sissay is a collection worth keeping close.'

Jack Rooke

'*The Dizziness of Freedom* is a thought-provoking and challenging
take on mental health conditions. It approaches the subject with
honesty, providing an important contribution to challenging the
stigma around mental health.'

Barbara Keeley, Shadow Cabinet Minister for Social Care and
Mental Health

The Dizziness of Freedom

Edited by Amy Acre and Jake Wild Hall

PRESS

The Dizziness of Freedom

Published by Bad Betty Press in 2018
www.badbettypress.com

Cover design by Lynne Eve

Printed and bound in the United Kingdom

A CIP record of this book is available from the British Library.

ISBN: 978-1-9997147-4-1

Supported using public funding by the National Lottery through Arts Council England

Supported using public funding by
**ARTS COUNCIL
ENGLAND**

Contents

The Dizziness of Freedom

In memory of Michael Clift

Foreword

The editors of this book approached me to write the introduction to this poetry anthology because, I suppose, I have been writing and speaking about mental distress for some time. I first entered a psychiatric in-patient unit at fourteen and have spent years of my life as an in-patient at various stages of my life. This does not qualify me to speak about the distress of others, or 'mental health' as a whole, but as an advocate for the importance of raising awareness of psychiatric conditions and mental distress, particularly when it concerns minority groups, children and teenagers and victims of trauma, I feel strongly that the work presented in this anthology is a powerful reminder that there is no one way to speak about distress. There is no one lexicon to use when speaking of it, and no person should be ignored when stepping through the threshold from silence to expression. After reading this anthology, I returned to a state of silence, though it was a most necessary state of reflection and witness.

The range of the poems in this book is vast, highlighting the non-universality of mental distress. Personally, I find the language of 'mental health' to be reductive, inadequate and damaging; for example, to use a word such as 'depression' as though it holds universal meaning negates the hugely varied experience of suffering. This book gives us individual insights into just how particular and nuanced the experiences of each human living with distress are and just how powerful language can be as a descriptive tool for such things as experience, consciousness, pain, suffering and enduring. There are similarities in some of the narratives in these poems – for example, David Turner in his poem 'John Dickson' writes of an experience of being an in-patient on a ward, being an observer whilst trapped in four walls where there is no universal or consistent idea of distress; where time expands and living space is reduced to distressed inhabitants and banal, ultra-ordinary objects. He writes, 'we laugh in unison as the egg timer is reset.' Salena Godden writes about a mother being taken from her home and children to a psychiatric unit, from the perspective of one of the children. The denouements are particularly sobering in both these poems, as they offer no conclusion or closure but instead help the reader to see inside experiences to which there were no other real witnesses to inner suffering. Both narratives capture an entirely different essence of the personal trauma of mental breakdown, whether it be as an onlooker, a dependant of a person who needs help, or as the distressed speaker, or as a combination of any of those – trapped inside themselves with their own turmoil, to some degree, whilst witnessing the difference of how turmoil presents in others. We are all trapped within the limits of our own consciousness, but the poets and poems in this book appear to have found a way out – allowing us to go there with them.

For me, the work of the poems in this anthology lies in their difference, their individuality, their shifting perspectives, their non-omnipotent narratives, their exemplary use of language to make distinctive steps towards elucidating what is so hard to explain in language. Poetry is beyond explanation, beyond language, it transcends the typical language of psychiatry; it opens wounds and allows cathartic transference between the reader and writer of a poem. The many experiences and emotions described or revealed in these poems are not didactic, there are remembered and examined ideas; captured thoughts and experiences that can offer no conclusion, they simply seek to lend a voice and a structure to what cannot be adequately explained. The poems in this anthology are exceptionally varied and far-reaching. It's especially true of these poems that the ways in and ways out – the titles and endings, are in themselves potent sources of catharsis and stirring echoes from the unconscious. Antosh Wojcik's title, 'Swimming cures mental illness, said no one, ever, in a doorway, picturing their dad, throwing himself down a staircase', is a maelstrom in itself, made only more intense by the poem, which uses its title as a counterpoint to an entirely internal maelstrom, explaining nothing yet revealing more than can be written or expressed in plain prose or lucid speech.

These poets have stepped outside themselves and beyond – to reveal something of the truth behind their own experience, expressing entirely unique and personal narratives, ideas, journeys, thoughts and identities. We are alive in an age in which there is more discourse and conversation regarding mental health, psychiatry and distress, though discourses are imperfect and care for those in need is seemingly reduced to a frighteningly inadequate level, as relayed in some of these poems. There have been many historical movements in recent times – the founding of psychoanalysis at the turn of the century, the insistence of 'care in the community' in the 60s, the abolition of the old mental asylums, the building of institutions for the young and for particular conditions such as eating disorders, the abolition of mixed sex psychiatric units, the uncovering of abuse scandals, the 'speaking out' of prominent figures and celebrities, the huge increase of use of pharmaceuticals and profiteering of pharmaceutical companies in the face of the apparent 'rise' in those experiencing psychiatric illness, the effect of austerity on mental health services, the closing of wards and reduction of numbers of beds. And here we are. What greater vehicle for understanding the current climate, its effects and its pitfalls, its abuses and its failings, its successes and its survivors than through language?

We have all, each of us, living today a tale to tell and an experience of our own to bear. The internet allows everyone to speak freely, to a degree, and to share their experience and the moments of their lives on social media; but it's clear that we are living in a time of extreme loneliness, actual poverty, spiritual poverty and a decline in compassion. Words and images fly at us so fast the effect can be highly desensitising; anyone with teenage children today will realise the huge difference in the way our children express themselves and have access to mobiles and the internet in often unhealthy ways. Poetry is a space in which sensitivity and sensibility hold still inside a structure; you can be in it and see inside it, but it has no universal way of being seen or understood. A poem can be a mode of survival, a message in a bottle, a key turning in a lock or the slamming of a door. Poetry is unsettling; it's not as accessible as a webpage or a blog, a magazine article or news report – it holds mystery and magic; and can bring a reader and writer into such proximity, the heart strains to hold the balance between the tension of the two. Poetry unlocks something of the unknown and turns the unrecognisable into something the other can recognise and confront. It gives others permission to express and feel things they might have thought taboo or unpalatable; it is a tool of anti-repression and a call to change. And it is the most beautiful of artforms, challenging and rewarding in the way it stirs and evokes something of the eternal and unconscious; far removed from being stuck in one moment in time, it takes an idea or image, dislodges the familiar representation of it, and takes us elsewhere. This anthology makes a bold proposition – it invites you to listen.

Melissa Lee-Houghton

Editor's Introduction

This book started life as a conversation between Jake Wild Hall and me in a living room in New Cross, when Bad Betty Press was brand new, before we knew if the idea would get any interest.

What we did know was that several of the poets we admired – Melissa Lee-Houghton, Byron Vincent, Emily Harrison, Rob Auton, Dean Atta and Luke Kennard to name a few – were writing about mental health in ways that seemed to reshape the conversation. They, and many writers we had yet to discover, were taking a subject historically defined by its otherness and talking about it with inclusivity and nuance, humanity and charm. We were irresistably drawn to the idea of compiling their work in a book we hoped would appeal not only to poetry fans but anyone interested in mental health. We wanted this book to be a bridge, connecting people suffering from any form of mental distress to others with similar stories, and to empowering language offering them a wider range of tools with which to speak out.

In the development of this book, it was truly educational to understand just how far and wide its subject carried meaning. Like the #metoo movement of the last 12 months, mental illness is having something of an 'I'm Spartacus' moment, with artists, celebrities and Facebook friends speaking out about their personal crises and recoveries, the illnesses they live with and those that sneak up on them. Concurrently, as more stories emerge about people's experiences with various healthcare systems, their strengths and shortcomings, there is a huge amount to learn about how we, as a society and as a world, can improve our response to mental ill health. I believe at the heart of this is the imperative to counter marginalising narratives pushed by the media and government, and acknowledge that the loss of mental health is one of the things that makes us most human.

Indeed, anxiety and despair are recognised as essential to the ontology of being human in Kierkegaard's *The Concept of Dread*, from which this book takes its title. Defining anxiety as 'the dizziness of freedom', he describes someone standing on the edge of an abyss, made dizzy by fear not of falling, but of jumping. Because to jump is a possibility, it stands in for the dizzyingly limitless possibilities that we face at each turn in life, including, of course, the possibility of our own destruction. If we become lost in vertigo, we may find ourselves drawn to the worst of our options, or else caught in an inertia which is just a different kind of death.

But the human condition is one thing. While feelings of panic and of sorrow, however they manifest, are universally familiar, we felt duty-bound, as editors, to interrogate if and where the boundaries lie between experiencing troubling emotions and identifying as 'mentally unwell', and to consider this carefully when choosing the writers we'd invite to contribute. We knew that if, say, a similar book about physical disabilities were to feature work by many able-bodied writers who had once broken a leg, it would, at the very least, be a point of contention. Most of us will go through a form of mental crisis at one point or other, but not everyone will be sectioned, spend time in an institution or be medicated either temporarily or for a lifetime, while others will. Some people lose jobs, partners or homes because of mental illness. Others live with difficulties that are primarily invisible, but that can nonetheless be a matter of life or death. We concluded that it was important for the book to reflect this vast range of types of experience as representatively and diversely as possible.

Of course, we didn't, and still don't, know the medical history of all our contributors. Of the 36 writers we initially contacted, the majority were already talking about mental health, either in their work or online. But we also asked some writers based purely on our esteem for their work, letting them decide whether or not they felt 'qualified' to speak on the subject. For the remaining 14 poets, we put out an open call for submissions, hoping to cast a net wider than our pond. This proved an effective way to discover both writers we didn't already know, and sides of some writers we did which were new to us. Reading submissions, we quickly learnt that we could easily publish at least a second book with the number of stirring, enlightening and vital poems we received. And while most of the work published here draws on firsthand experience, there are also many stories about living with the illness, and in some cases, loss, of a friend or loved one – stories just as necessary to tell. In fact, the more time we spent with the subject, the clearer it became that there is no one kind of story about mental health. There are as many as there are people.

Nonetheless, in an attempt to give the reader some orientation, we've loosely categorised the work into chapters. We wanted to avoid psychiatric labels and instead, group poems based on an experience or feeling in common. To do this, we've borrowed some of the lavish and inspired titles that our contributors gave to their poems, such as Pascal Vine's 'all the holes you want to fill are already full of sky' and Caleb Femi's 'At A House Party, *Ultralight Beam* Came On & It Started A Church Service' – titles that, as well as depicting a feeling or moment, offer a great preview of our authors' humour, linguistic talent and lateral thinking.

To make the poems in this book more accessible, we've included links to video and audio recordings of as many of them as possible. These appear both as written links and QR codes which can be read by pointing a smartphone camera at the code. (See the Accessibility Guide on page 17 for more details.)

We hope this book will go some way to furthering everyday conversation about what's happening on the inside, that it will reach people who feel alone and encourage them to speak out, and that it will act as a reminder that the subject of mental health is relevant to everyone.

We are immensely grateful to all our contributors, who have been generously honest and brave in sharing their stories. I would like to extend particular thanks to my co-editor, Jake Wild Hall, to Melissa Lee-Houghton who wrote the foreword, and to Arts Council England, who made this book possible.

Amy Acre

Accessibility Guide

Some of our authors have kindly provided video or audio recordings of their poems, as alternative ways to access the work. We've put them into online playlists which can be found here:

Video
tinyurl.com/y9e5cnxk

Audio
tinyurl.com/y8dryrbs

QR Codes
You can also link to recorded content directly from the individual poems. Poems that have an online recording have a QR code after them. A QR code looks like this:

Point a smartphone camera at a QR code and you'll receive a notification with a link to the rcording. The one above takes you to our YouTube playlist.

Here's one for Soundcloud:

If you don't have access to a smartphone, please type the links on the previous page into a URL bar to navigate through the playlists.

"I long ago abandoned the notion of a life without storms, or a world without dry and killing seasons."

Kay Redfield Jamison

"He whose eye happens to look down the yawning abyss becomes dizzy. It is just as much in his own eye as in the abyss, for suppose he had not looked down. Hence, anxiety is the dizziness of freedom, which emerges when the spirit wants to posit the synthesis and freedom looks down into its own possibility, laying hold of finiteness to support itself."

Søren Kierkegaard

all the holes you want to fill are
already full of sky

Bobby Parker

Zippo

I asked the knife to guide me through council estates in the rain.
I didn't give a shit about the suffering of animals.
I would squint my eyes at teachers and imagine their faces
rotting away like B-movie Zombies. I hand-delivered creepy letters
to the houses of popular girls from my class who reminded me
of the dolls on my mother's bedside table. I faked asthma attacks
to get out of doing sports. The first time I examined my testicles
I cried all night, convinced they were full of poisonous,
microscopic fish. Doesn't it break your heart when the snow
won't stick? Another broken promise. It makes me feel like a witch.
When my mother caught me stealing from her purse she
dragged me by the hand, screaming, towards the glowing cooker.
I walked as slowly as possible up the hill and saw my dad's face
in the window like a troubled king, waiting to whip my ass
with his leather belt. In all fairness, it didn't hurt a bit; I grinned
into the fluffy quilt, thinking about all the other things
I could get away with. Once, standing by a river with my
erect cock out, enjoying the autumn wind, a girl appeared
carrying a bag filled with muddy high-heeled shoes,
which she threw at me. I kept a stash of weapons
in my school locker: pellet guns, smoke bombs, knives;
I had a reputation for being a little psycho, which was only
half true, a phase I hope to purge. The deputy head teacher
would make me sit in his office while he ate a whole bunch
of large bananas. When a boy called Ryan spat in my face,

I followed him to the park where he sat on the grass
with his back to me. I took a long run up and kicked his head
like a football, knocking him unconscious, then I ran home and hid
in my wardrobe, waiting for the police to come and arrest me
for murder. The first naked woman I saw in a dirty magazine
at the back of the playing field was mixed race, so was my first
girlfriend. She was not a magazine. It took a lot of practice.
Mother told me that boys have a tail and girls have a hole.
That's it. Nothing about love, pleasure, intimacy. Just tails
going into holes, creating potential monsters like me. I watched
my grandad slowly lose his mind with grief and whisky.
After nan died he would scream at the living room wall for days
while Pavarotti boomed from the speakers of his dusty radio,
drowning out the horrific tinnitus he developed during the war.
My best friend helped me dig under my grandad's shed
searching for dinosaur bones. We found two small skulls
which I cleaned and brought into science class, only to be told
they were the remains of cats, hence my short-lived reputation
as a cat killer. Thankfully, I discovered poetry, it was my secret;
it excited me. I was sent to the warehouse above Marks & Spencer
for work experience, where I groped the cold, white breasts of
headless mannequins and all I could think about was stealing
women's stockings, black, shiny, secretly wearing them
as I jerked off in the toilets. But I could never go through with it.
I was convinced that every person to ever die and go to Heaven
was watching me, appalled. Since my dad is a Glazier
there were always odd bits of glass laying around the house.
His thumbs loosely wrapped with oozing bandages.
I enjoyed squishing slugs and snails between two small pieces

of broken glass, so that I could see the colours of their insides.
Whenever dad left the room I would use his brass Zippo lighter
to burn the faces off my favourite action figures. There was
a very odd woman who lived down the street, her name
was Mandy, she had intense silver eyes and wore pink wool
jumpers that were way too big for her but made her seem
closer to my age at the time. Mandy invited me into her house,
she let me feel her big tits. The way she growled and licked
her lips disturbed me. I took the Dictaphone I got
for my twelfth birthday to the local haunted house
and propped it up in the fire-damaged kitchen, hoping
to catch something supernatural. When I retrieved it
the next day, the Dictaphone had recorded the voice of a boy
begging a girl to suck his dick, the sound of a scuffle, gagging,
sobbing. I believed the Devil was playing tricks on me.
If I could choose between complete sobriety or self-discipline
I would choose the willpower to enjoy drugs occasionally
without my life falling apart and disappointing my family.
This is subject to change. Do you have to write about yourself
to make sense of yourself? I don't know anything about you.
Tell me. I'm becoming a real creature of the moment.
Have you considered writing a diary from the perspective
of your genitalia? My earliest memory of being truly aware
of my penis, I was sat on a bed behind the curtains
with our family doctor, he was rolling my foreskin up and down
for a long time. Right now, it feels creepy crawly,
which always happens when it knows it's being talked about.
Hidden in my dad's bedside drawer was a poem he wrote
for my mother when she was pregnant with me, in hospital,

awaiting chemotherapy for the cancer that appeared in her neck
like a hundred baked beans under the skin. He wrote about
how he couldn't wait to meet their baby daughter. Perhaps
this was the first seed. I had already been through stages
when I believed I was an alien, sent to cause chaos.
If this is the wrong body, I thought, I'll fucking ruin it.
A posh boy who lived in the big house on the hill asked me
to use his camcorder to record a video of him masturbating.
When I refused, he threw biscuits at the Au Pair until she took off
crying down the road and got hit by a bus. I think about her
whenever I eat Vegan breakfasts. Early memories, for me,
can often be summed up with one chilling sentence.
If you had to describe your childhood in terms of food,
what lunch would you be? I was a cold Happy Meal.
The only time I think about my doomed wedding day,
I see my ex-wife and I, posing for pictures in front of St Mary's,
the greenish stone archway covered with hundreds of Ladybirds,
dropping into her veil and crawling all over her white dress.
It was magical. According to legend, in France,
if a Ladybird lands on you, whatever ailment you have
will fly away with the Ladybird. In some Asian cultures
it is believed that Ladybirds understand human language
and have been blessed by God. I couldn't consummate
the marriage because I was too high on strong biker speed.
We watched cartoons until we fell asleep. Do you ever
put your thumb in your mouth and run the tip of your tongue
across your thumbnail to appreciate how smooth and glassy it is?
In some areas, this is a signal to a dark, twisted figure
in a second-floor hotel window. Do we really die?

I do not recommend loneliness, though I know many people
can enjoy their own company without going slightly insane.
I am not one of these people. I slap my own face so hard
my teeth rattle. I do this because I feel lost in all the noise
of apparent normalcy. The day you were born
is essentially the most important thing to happen ever.
Remember this when someone tries to convince you
to do something disgusting. Remember this when governments
fall and wolves are reintroduced to the English countryside.
Remember this: your physical presence can be reduced
to a drop of digital blood falling through eternal screens.
In this I have achieved a small release. I live easier for a while.
Maybe I am to blame for the way her life turned out.
My passion for drugs was predestined, handed down
like a broken watch, inevitable as flies. My heart
was like the Bermuda Triangle: birds fell out of the sky
and loved ones vanished in the dead of night. Then I got clean.
Finally a good father, fighting to protect my daughter
whose mother says the reason she's with another fucked-up addict
in the first place is because I normalised that way of life for her,
so it should be no surprise she's now in love with a man
who does the same shit I did only a hundred times worse.
When the guilt is really bad it's like my skull picks up
all these wild vibrations, echoes, songs, stories, voices,
instruments, animal noises, soundtracks to German cinema.
In the absence of faith or spirituality (which I once had in abundance)
I struggle to see beyond the poorly packaged bacon of existence.
Katy tells me science is beautiful and pure. Sometimes I believe her.
Now we're past the church I can't hear anything but rain.

I'm jeepers creepers in love again. Is it true you can enter
other people's dreams and cast a sickness upon them?
I heard people who die angry can become powerful ghosts.
I memorised the names of antidepressants as if they were angels.
I threw my illness off a bridge and ran as fast as I could.

Ruth Sutoyé

Clockwork

6:12pm – B

She soldiers in first minutes after a dipping sun
takes her place in ritual on ceramic floor
head prostrating over toilet bowl in reverence.
Two forefingers readied for sacrifice
down
they
go
deep
                                   then finally kneeling.
Pouring up the vodka, following on   apple crumble custard-less,
following on   pad thai.
She hears the footsteps at the door become ghosts.

1:15pm – K

Pantry has a way of doubling up as heaven
(With its singular activity – consumption).

Cakebiscuitsbeefpattiesvodkamorecakevodkachickenmarrowvodkaplantain
garlicbreadhalloumivodkaicecreamvodkavodkavodkavodka.

Heaven's best: Two pops of Bisacodyl.

8:27pm – B

Back to ritual
an expectant moon, the floor
the swords in throat
down
they
go
deep.
The phone, left ringing abruptly halts
even in silence, the room murmurs and croons.

Her cavities are eroding boulders.
Mirror tells her herbreasts are bedrock
a whale's back are hertorsoandhips,
hernose a hippo's face in mourning.

She performs the ritual again for good measure.

Fran Lock

confessions of a hunger artist

incurably polluted shape, i now renounce. friday is a parable
of calcites. cortisonal sea i swim, too light to drown. he whittled
this body from green wood. it is his body, not mine. i have no
body. i want nobody. god cannot help me, all his remedy is
cleanliness, and i will never be clean; no pasteurised epiphany
will wash this dirt away. i'm staging my erasure in a baggy
shirt instead. don't look at me. i'm twisting like a pencil in
the corner of your eye. i have no desire to be desired. i've no
desire at all. and i repent this blatant flesh, would live, without
sustenance or compromise. intake, ideation, anything measured.
it's not about beauty. there's a cinder inside, and the pain
encrusts it, accreting a pearl. i'll make a weapon of this
emptiness, so sharp that you could cut yourself. meticulous
sickness i wear like a uniform. guerrilla girl with gritted teeth.

Jake Wild Hall

blank

blank
wake up
fall asleep
blank
pick it up
put it down
i shouldn't
but why
you're missing the point
blank
back to the start
when was the start
i am losing my days
it's fine
no it's not
blank
roll
then again
fine
then again
try this
it has no effect
blank
sleep is cause and effect
blank

it has no effect
no more relief
maybe this is the end
roll
blank
roll
then again
fine
then again
try this
it has no effect
blank
wake up
fall asleep
blank
pick it up
put it down
i shouldn't
but why
you're missing the point
blank
sleep is cause and effect
blank
back to the start
when was the start
i am losing my days
it's fine
no it's not
blank

it has no effect
no more relief
maybe this is the end
help
clarity

the first time you feel this it will be infinite
not in a good way
your day will drag like fingernails on chalkboards
you will ask yourself why the sun in a clear sky is ugly
the morning will be an itch you can't scratch
human contact a necessity
the sun will go down
stars will come out
the heavens will be empty

at this point you will in one way or another start again

Dominic Berry

Men Locked Behind Toilet Doors

Jack and Ben are men locked behind a toilet door. Jack is fucking Ben's arse. The air is hot and smells of vomit. Ben knows Jack owns every Bjork CD even the remix ones yes even the shit remix ones. Ben's shit is on Jack's legs and inside Jack's boxer shorts. Ben thinks, *Don't stop.* Never. Be. Lonely. The sound of half a phone call is heard outside. Another man explains to someone else that he needs it Thursday not Friday *no it has to be Thursday no listen it must be Thursday no you don't understand Thursday Thursday fuck.* Ben thinks, *Don't stop.* Great pain. Jack does not know Ben's name. Jack adores the taste of his own sweat *mmm yes* he licks his upper lip *mmm yes* he wishes someone was filming him right now xtube this is love *mmm yes* this could go viral.

Tom is alone. Locked behind a toilet door. It is nine days until Tom's 14th birthday. The air smells of bleach. Never. Be. Lonely. *Thump* someone's boot kicks the outside of the toilet door *come out queer fucking queer I'm going to get you fucking queer fucking queer fuck you queer fuck you.* Tom does not know if he is gay. Tom knows this is fear. Will never leave. He will die. *Thump* Tom knows that there will never be a day when he won't be a man locked behind some toilet door *come out fucking queer.* Tom. Can't. Cry.

William is locked behind a toilet door. They made him play as the fat guy in *Mortal Kombat X.* No one likes the fat guy in *Mortal Kombat X.* He wants to be a Thunder God. Would settle for a ninja but they made him play as the fat guy in *Mortal Kombat X.* Fat guy spits fat balls of puke. *Use fingers* William. *Special moves* William. Quarter circle down throat down down left right purge. William no longer chokes on chunks will often use his toothbrush today it's only fingers it's almost like thin lightning bolts splat pattern porcelain. Milkshake. Waffles. Scrambled egg. *Splat splat splat.* One day he will be God of Thunder. Never. Be. Lonely and don't tell mum and don't tell mum and don't tell mum and don't tell mum and don't tell mum.

Dan is a man locked behind a toilet door. Yes. Cocaine-caked nostrils. Yes. Dan's atoms are sexy dancing high kicks. Yes. Dan's mum wouldn't know a sexy atom not if she saw one do the splits. Dan's friend outside, *I'll be ok in a minute mate, I'll be ok in a minute mate fuck off mate* Dan's atoms are vibrating exploding shaking their groove thang what kind of lame arse atoms do you have anyway mate there are disco atoms in Dan's dick and there are disco atoms in Dan's fist and there are tingly sharp atoms in Dan's disco nose. Never. Be. Lonely. Dan knows

it is not on top of Tibetan mountains. Nirvana is here. Dan has never heard a remix album by Bjork. Dan unlocks his toilet door. Steps outside and Dan. Can. Breathe. Fuck. Dan. Can. Breathe.

Melissa Lee-Houghton

Heroin

My friend, some desolation is so self-explanatory you are doing a
disservice to language to describe it. And mine was
riddled up to the neckline in sweat-rimmed viognier, post-editorial
meeting, sinus-suicide cocaine, summoning the will to go home and sleep
as people do every day so I've heard; instead
                              you see I knew what was coming so I
met it on the incline. Some weeks I can actually taste the pain before it
arrives –
my heroin addiction is economically viable and actually quite banal, which
seems a shame. As far as rituals go it's just so perfect I'm sorry to say –
dealers take longer about it, and I realised last week I have no sense of
time whatsoever, never think of it until I'm waiting to score down an
alleyway.

Seconds blur to a halt in reverse. Some days I lie in bed purring. I lie
uncomfortably and can't be bothered to move. The itching doesn't bother
me; my whole body
infested with histamines and bliss; and I scratch myself for hours, and talk
myself out of the value of intellect. Or Love, or liberty.
Never so enslaved as to this drug. Writhing all the way to Euston, back
twinges, shakes, sweat and orangina. Is it realistic

to want to suffer less. I don't screw grandmothers over. I think up a reality
TV show in which I train dealers to be better at their job;
food that is not even food sustains nonetheless; if I smoke it my lungs will

forgive me in time for my shortness of breath I watch comedy shows with my eyes closed and the world is on hold so tomorrow I will eat ice cream if I have to eat. That'll sort it. Yes.

Celebrated poet my arse. One breast and a desire to elope with the first person who loves me slightly more than their cat or their more 'stable' spouse.
I watch the sun rise and sun set as a counterpoint to how much do I need to set me right. My managerial life decisions make the ebbs easier to overlook.
Fucks sake I thought I'd outrun the smack. Too honest to be really good at it. And that first hit will never cease to weaken me at the knees.

No you'll never live up to it. You know the cons but do you know the pros?
Heroin is the best lover I ever had and he doesn't even care if I drool. He doesn't care if I vomit. He thinks being incapacitated is elegant. I apply red lipstick at regular intervals life darkens to a wound that ever fills with pus. They're saying

I'll live. Mouth around the tube. Never had reason to buy candles or cottonfloss. I wish I'd never seen anything better than this.
I wish I didn't sit around stoned watching the better things exist; you have no right
to happiness. I wish you had any idea. No, I have no real home and I'm fine.

Monsieur.
I have no answer.
My veins plead for the sanctity in I no longer give a fuck.

Pascal Vine

all the holes you want to fill are already full of sky

I've been thinking about sucking a friend's cock a lot lately.

But when I do
I feel like I'm falling.
I feel like that's the kind of thing I should tell a therapist and not an audience, but my obsessive compulsive disorder isn't visible normally.

I like sex.
I like to feel safe.
Sex isn't about that. Because of the whole, the brain is the biggest sex organ thing.
I've always thought the atmosphere is bigger, turns out I'm a god of turning weather, of restless clouds making wet decisions and my cliffside skin is my altar.

It's not a fall without adrenaline, it's not sex unless you had to double check you that you liked it.
And yet.
I still kinda wanna suck my friend's cock.

I'd also like to see the ground coming,
let the earth give me a courtesy shoulder tap,
before I break every bone in my body when I text him, hands shaking, the next day, "Yeah, I had fun, I promise, again some time".

It is okay to want to soar and never want to leave its embrace, it's okay to be confused, it's okay to be enthusiastic, it's okay to be hurt – past tense. It's okay to not want to conserve space in your bed by having someone go through you, it's okay to stop if you feel translucent, it's okay to have no room for anything but trust and the naturally occurring heavens in your abdomen.

It's okay to let tinder dates down to just end up spooning and sharing your skymiles and angels with anyone who asks you
because they never learnt the value of a good rejection, or found themselves floating in the serenity of a cancelled commitment.

Whatever you have to do to stick that landing, do it, I forgive myself for trying for a happy ending,
Because, sometimes, I feel like falling –

Maria Ferguson

Body

Body is problematic.
Body is hungry but scared of eating.
Body is beautiful,
only when somebody says that it is
but body is living.

Body is singing itself to sleep
on a cold night in February.
Body is giving a speech
to a room full of people
with spinach in its teeth.

Body is trying on all the clothes
it bought from ASOS
and giving a front room catwalk
to the cat.

Body is getting bigger,
and smaller, and bigger
again, but body is
starting to accept that.

Body will eat in public now.
Body will have sex with the lights on.
Body will try on jeans in a shop changing room

and won't take it too personally if they don't fit.

If body doesn't fit in to old clothes
it buys new ones,
it doesn't shrink.

Body is trying very hard to be well.
Body is going to the gym, sometimes,
if it feels like it.
Body is moisturising every night,
and enjoying the feel of itself.

Body is starting to think
that it might be possible to fall in love
with another body, but only when
Body is beautiful, without somebody
saying it is.

The day is all over me until I
find that place

Lemn Sissay

Quiet Places

Some people on bus seats shake at the shoulders,
Stoned Elvises trying to dance after the gig.

Some walk into the rain and look like they're smiling,
Running mascara writes sad bitter letters on their faces.

Some drive their cars into lay-bys or park edges
And cradle the steering-wheel looking like headless drivers.

Some sink their open mouths into feather pillows
And tremble on the bed like beached dolphins.

Some people are bent as question marks when they weep
And some are straight as exclamation marks.

Some are soaking in emotional dew when they wake,
Salt street maps etched into their faces.

Some find rooms and fall to the floor as if praying to Allah.
    Noiseless
Faces contorted in that silent scream that seems like laughter.

Why is there not a tissue-giver? A man who looks for tears,
Who makes the finest silk tissues and offers them for free?

It seems to me that around each corner, beneath every stone,
Are humans quietly looking for a place to cry on their own.

Mary Jean Chan

Dragon Hill Spa

Seoul, South Korea

It is the year 2016, but you know
how women tame their own bodies

into bones, dig their own graves in
daylight. Here, for once, in a hot bath

of rainbows, the bodies let themselves
go, the water holds them up to the light,

the lips murmur a prayer to skin. Here,
the only hands that touch their wrists

are their own. Here is no-man's land.
Here, the names of soldiers, heavy-

handed, are forgotten. Here, no one
takes what they want from the women

whose gods are freely chosen,
whose bones are theirs to bury.

Raymond Antrobus

The day is all over me until I find that place

that beach, those feet, that blue, that air,
the moment that is and is not breathing
and I know how hard it is to get into the spot
that says *sleep*
            it is ok, you are safe, your mother
is coming home, your father is already dead.
He no longer needs comfort, not while
I'm here with another cupboard
and a set of clothes to put on
to walk around in
                    like everyone with two arms,
legs and a heartbeat. I can't make importance out of
sense. Can't make sense of the turning
and the losing of myself, and finding
the kind of universe where people sit
crossed-legged under bridges and spit
into rivers. In my head
I am sitting down too. This is how far I have
to come away from myself   to be with myself.
To know that breath always finds its depth
in the calm ground of every
earthly
        silence.

Rob Auton

Lifelines and Landlines

Is this what I feel like when I'm happy?
I'm enjoying pulling these weeds from the gravel
The sound design is faultless
Unseen understone breaking of roots
How could I be more content?
If the weeds weren't here with me?
Would that improve my mood?
I wouldn't think about the weeds if they were not here for me to work on
I've got my brown suede slippers on
I only came down this shed end for a look
Now I've got a pile on the go
Grey dry dirt finger ends doing what they were meant for

It's Monday morning in October
I've just seen the frantic underbelly of a woodlouse
Resuscitated fossil
Full of levers and bars
Lead in colour
Should be stone but woodlice are made from themselves and brilliance
Legs and arms without a need for feet or hands

What more do I need than this goalkeeper-free weed goal?
People applauding me for enjoying myself?
How could I feel more successful when pulling up a weed?
I could have a gardener doing it for me

He or she would find me when he or she has done it
Having achieved what I could have
My phone is in the house just like it was in my parent's garden
I love being outside with empty pockets
These weeds are landlines
And mental stability is ringing me on them

Rob Auton

Doors

One door closes, another door... closes.
One door closes, another door opens and another door closes.
One door opens, another door opens, another door opens, another door
opens, another door opens, then five more doors open but you are too
slow making your decision so they all simultaneously slam in your face.
One door opens, another door closes, one door opens and you jump
through it then look back at the door and see that it is shut again.
You want to get back through but you can't.
You look around for other doors but there are only doorframes in this new
environment that you are in. Why walk through a doorframe?
Suddenly the doorframes have doors and you really want to walk through
them now but you can't because they all have signs on them and the
signs say CLOSED and you don't question the signs. You could check
the doors but you are too busy thinking about a new shiny door that is
surrounded by light bulbs like a mirror in Dolly Parton's dressing room.

One door opens, another door closes, another door opens, another door
opens but you ignore them all because you are focused on this door. The
Dolly door. This is the door. This is the door to your future. The one you
need to get through more than any other. After this door every other door
will just be a door. You bang on the Dolly door until the Dolly door opens
and Dolly Parton is there and she's got doors for eyes and a door for a
nose and small black doors for nostrils and a double door for a mouth and
hundreds of yellow doors for hair and you can't decide which of Dolly's
doors you want to go through. Her eyes open and shut like they are

53

blinking at you, you think she is flirting so you walk through her mouth and you instantly wish you had gone through her nose. You are in her mouth and her tongue is a fleshy pink trapdoor, her teeth are white doors and you think about all these new doors that could open to you but you just stand there and hope that they open for you instead of kicking them down.

One door opens, another door opens, another door closes, you find someone who is looking for the same doors as you, you begin to walk through the doors together and it isn't quite as hard as before. You find humour in the doors, you find love in the doors, you find children in the doors, you find life in the doors. One door closes, another door opens, and the lid of your coffin slams shut.

Another door opens and you are in Heaven and all the doors in front of you are open. You start to think about how good it was to have closed doors.

Doors with something behind them.

Roddy Lumsden

Written While Weepy

Since there are such things as charge us:
bulls of doubt, the nightmare promising,
baby rabbits dashing on forgotten graves,
we need the solid of our selves to rope

what future we have left. To lie alone
and imagine an embrace; to curtsey
to our own abandon. Late hours dither
then whack us. I do not want that thought.

The colours which do not suit us gather
and regulate. What I am after is some safe.
Just simpleness. Sea, perhaps, or guessing.
Road home. The pulse of the immediate.

I cry because I am. There will be no sorry.
If I look at you, it is because I need to look.
Look. The burr has caught on my clothes.
I swipe at it. Only that way the night may end.

Joel Auterson

Fingers

I've got Virgil on hold again. He's heard Someone Like You
twenty-eight times and he's still on the line. I admire his
breath control. Most of these winters my body is an excuse
for itself. In the mornings I apologise to each of my teeth in
turn and try to convince my fingers it's worth the effort. My
left ear hates Decembers and I can't stop thinking about how
the *clapping* and *praying* emojis are almost identical. I've
been told I worry people. I've been told I look worried. I've
been told it's entirely possible that I will never again be this
essential. I've been *told* that a twist has to come with a
shout, that a wick can stretch so far a flame won't take, that
certain knowledge will lose to uncertain threat *every single
time.*

The sixth winter is retreating when I leave Virgil behind at
the foot of the stairs.
It's not freedom, not really.
However.

R.A. Villanueva

Saudade

Yes now, like you, I wonder: where
is the patron saint of exiles
and far districts, this prefecture
of salt licks, pollen? Of alleys

blue with plaques? And who among those
martyrs gives the nieces we have
yet to hold close our faces to
learn, our names to try? Who will halve

our pills for us, heat the bacon
fat, steep the tea? Everywhere wine
and moss. Everywhere fog. *The wrecks
of ships around the Whitefish Point*

and bodies the lake won't give back,
you say: *like that — a love like that.*

a backward dark

Katie Metcalfe

The Pale Fox

The sun has yet to unfurl his backbone,
but my father is already out, climbing
the big hill towards the woods.

I watch him through my bedroom window.

I can see his lips moving. He curses the sky,
her many tongues of drizzle.

It was yesterday the news came
of a pale fox, fur and eyes
white as elderflowers.

My father is in the woods for hours, coming home
as dusk is settling the sun in her lap.

The pale fox is over his shoulder.
I can see her eyes from a quarter of a mile away.

I imagine how her senses would have ignited
as my father approached the den.

She would have smelt his sour scent
as it emerged through the undergrowth.

Her entire body would have been arrow pointed.

You shouldn't have taken her, my mother says,
mashing tea. *The woods won't like it.*
You should have let her be.

He ignores her. He always does.

But my mother grew up with one foot in the furrows,
one foot in the forest. She knows the land,
she's tasted the roots of its mysteries.

There is much boasting as mother cleans
father's bait box, pours the tea,
folds the kitchen cloths into neat squares
with her eyes closed.

****

I follow the sharp tang of death
back to a silent den.

I find them, the cubs, tiny and white,
clutched together in a knot of soft fur,
small teeth, dry blood.

Maggots are already crawling in their eyes.

I wonder about the father.
Is he running back over the hills to home,
oblivious, a fat pheasant between his teeth?

I gently move the cubs from the entrance,
back down into the earth they were born onto.
They are still slightly supple.

I fill the den,
locking them deep within.

I wonder if the father will dig them out.
I wonder if he will scream tonight.

****

My father has the pale fox taxidermied
before the weekend is over.

He stands her in the hallway.

Her eyes are preserved in formaldehyde.
He has them on the mantelpiece.

My father and his friends drink whisky
from crystal glasses.

My mother dips candles
and dries lavender.

My father and his friends stroke the fox's back,
call her 'the foolish white bitch.'

Father talks of how he strangled her
so as not to stain her coat.

I imagine how she lifted her lips
back over her teeth, until her last, brave breath.

Father tells his friends that in Finland,
the aurora borealis is known as fox fires,
because in the far north it's thought foxes
paint the skies with their tails.

He tells his friends that the Celts
honoured the fox for its wisdom.

I told him of these things.

They laugh, holding their guts, tears swarming.
They talk about the forthcoming hunt,
for the copper brothers and sisters of the pale fox.

****

The fever starts unexpectedly.
Father goes to bed for days.

She was in here, with her cubs,

at the bottom of the bed, she was there
and they were all screaming, they were all screaming!

He talks of nothing but the foxes.

The pale fox and her cubs come every day.
Soon my father is messing himself, hiding
under his covers, a quivering mountain.

The smell of shit takes over the whole house.

The fox's body still stands in the hallway,
a formidable woodland queen.

I bury her one night, just inside the woods.
I wish for her peace over my father's.

As father dies, he makes one hideous noise
after another, until fading into silence.

The swollen green jewels of his eyes turn milky,
and pale fox cubs chase their tails around his bed,
while the mother sits atop his chest
and cleans herself.

Caleb Femi

East Dulwich Road

When a knife enters you, there will be no pain.
People on the street & on buses will stare
as if witnessing a natural phenomenon.
They will imagine the pain they think you are in
but you will feel none at all.

You will question if you have always been
an empty cove waiting to be filled by another boy's rage.
Whether this is how mutation works, after many generations
your black body now comfortably accepts the blade
like an inheritance -a birthmark on your obsidian torso.

Rachel Nwokoro

Muscle Memory

there are memories
with legs
that know how to chase
that have discovered how to survive in
inhospitable environments
that have learnt to endure
what
you
cannot

there are memories with legs
that search for you

legs
that you would rather break
than touch

Claire Trévien

Daytime Drinking Brain

I hope it doesn't end up	[end]
in one of your poems,	[your poems]
he says.	[he says]
Give me a coaster	[give me]
and I will create	[I will create]
strange confetti, a dagger.	[a dagger]
Rape is so cliché.	[so cliché]
Oh I had a bad experience	[experience]
and now it fills all my words	[my words]
with paralysis and smoke	[smoke]
and *the trauma of it*	[of it]
Yes, I agree, quite enough	[quite enough]
already from other…	[from others]
The pub is intricate like	[like]
a chocolate box – and	[a box]
just as lacquered	[lacquered]
and you came back	[and]
wrong.	[wrong]

Mary Jean Chan

Rise and Shine

This morning your voice is a cleft wing and the sky
is all echo. The therapist says *Avoid the foetal position
because there will be too much blood
concentrated around the vital organs* –

by which she means *Try to sit up
and greet the day anew.* When air becomes a cage.
When breathing demands concentration:
a striving of muscle and sinew.

When syllables transmute into blabber, hiccup,
torrent leaking from every orifice on your devastated face.
Your voice is a river running deep underground.
Your lover asks for language, and you cannot give it.

Last night the faucet broke, and you cursed the water
for failing you. You have had enough
of water, that embryonic fluid that broke you
onto this patch of earth, screaming

and alone. Water reminds you of your mother's
grief, so you down three glasses and wish the icecaps
across the Arctic would flood the world into oblivion.
Your lover's voice is so utterly ordinary

in its pain that you could almost empathise.
How did we survive? You whisper this
into her breasts, her hands smoothing your brow,
her voice in your ears like weather.

Kat François

They Say

They say we turned out well
so we laugh at our own trauma,
sharing stories of childhood beatings,
excusing abuse
with talk of
discipline and culture.

They say we turned out well
so we allow our elders to pacify us with tales
of the harsh discipline dished out 'Back-home'
that their small bodies received,
gifted by their Caribbean parents,
a gift they happily passed on.

They say we've turned out well
because of the
cold, hard
slaps, pinches,
licks and lashes,
their 'Beat first, talk later' mantra.

They say we've turned out well
because of the strict upbringing
and the boundaries
pulled rope-tight around us,

and that no real harm
was done, only good.

They say we've turned out well
as they try to soothe our adult questioning
with strong laments of
'We had it so much worse'
and try to dampen our anger
with talk of 'You're lucky you weren't raised in the West Indies.'

They say we've turned out well
and so we joke
and nod in agreement,
complicit in
the romanticisation
of our own abuse.

Nicki Heinen

#metoo

This skin dries bloodless, underneath a ghost slip scratches pale blue
feather in my mouth turns liquid like tide pods exploding
the sun is absent, a carnation wilts on the grave, a shadow not falling
no crater so deep as the hole in my mind, filled with all the things I said
all the things you took, all the things undone
furniture of the bipolar kingdom, stuffed full of dust mites
burrowing in like spinning tops
Is it not an exercise set for the next time?
No, it's not
It's this moment in which I stand
a woman enfettered
stand with my feather in my mouth
my blood on your lips, your face etched in the winter air
my head splintering, a silent grenade

Anne Gill

Green trauma bear

At the clinic they give out green trauma bears; *this will make you feel safe.*
The green trauma bears are silent and green and have sharp claws encased
in bubble wrap to stop accidents. The green trauma bears are gentle and
dusty. They are about half the size of a lamp-post. It is understood that they
will help. It is understood that *this will make you feel safe.*

They do not help. Subject 1 still exhibits symptoms of anxiety when walking
down the road at night even though a green trauma bear follows, plodding
methodically, at a safe distance. Subject 2 does not seem to notice its green
trauma bear and Subject 3 pops all the bubbles on the bubble wrap on the
claws of its green trauma bear and then holds the green trauma bear's paw
in place and scores their arm along the now freed claws. The green trauma
bear sighs and does not react. The green trauma bear is just doing its job
which, quite frankly, it is not prepared for.

The green trauma bear must follow the Subject wherever it goes like a
shadow. The Subject does not feel safe. The Subject does not feel safe. Subject
12 uses a green trauma bear as a ladder to scale the fence by the railway
line before implanting itself on the track. A green trauma bear follows like
a concerned parent. A green trauma bear follows like a shadow. A green
trauma bear follows even though it would probably rather be playing pool
right now. A green trauma bear follows.

Fran Lock

a backward dark

i grew like a twisted tooth, and every day was a backward dark, and delving awkward into morning, met by soft syndromal light let into rooms through cracks in glass and gaps in brick. how should i spend *my precious time?* these hours of stricken and hiccuping mien, and what did *you think would happen?* left alone to my own gaunt indifference, with nothing to get up for. they said they could not help me, professional obsessives in the glum and underfunded rooms i crawled to and then back, by ugly alleyways and flats, breathing in an air of eager menace; psychotic riposte, urine and homicidal shoplift. inside, a dead, dry plant with crispy bacon leaves, expired medication. they said they could not help me. i am less than nothing, an excrescence in the eye of an overworked gp. what should i do? slump my misshapen shoulders at the desk, survive on sheepish chivalries, the profligate affinities of friends who say they love me and then do not call for days? or drag my debt to be the subject of slack whispers in the local bar, to hide from crowds of people with my old cowering proficiency. an online forum told me *you are not your worst day,* but this disease puts out more roots than branches, and anyway, there's nowhere left to go but down. they said they could not help me. grey-brown fish food flakes of snow. my mirror is a study in malnourishment. i drop my untidy shadow by the bed like crumpled clothes. i *try* to work, at anything at all. i do not want to live like this, prostrate before the bailiffs yet again. i do not want to live. a book is better eaten than drowned. evicted, unemployable, people like *me shouldn't aim too high.* it's friday and the blackly estimated self is slipping. i wish this pain electric, to exit via the fingertips in sparks. but it does not, it is a dull and stumbling blow, the cold slap of another wave. this pain makes nothing. it's all i'm good for, born for, groomed to droop, to wheedle in a stuttering rank to clinics and to agencies, and *what is wrong with you?* burning up with shame, it's red-faced sensibility. in university i learnt to tell *suffering* from *punishment*, for all the good that's done me. i grew like a twisted tooth, with dirt at the crown and rot at the root.

are stars supposed to move like
that

Sean Wai Keung

are stars supposed to move like that

the thing they dont
tell you about delusions is when they stop
so that even if you now know
its unrealistic to think
there are satellites tracking my movements

you dont know how real
istic it is to think
i am the greatest living poet
which means you are

always doubting
yourself but trust me

those satellites cant see through clouds
+ there are always darker places for you
to hide out there

Byron Vincent

WOT

And the earth split

like a nest of spider eggs

And the cheers scuttled out, as sincere as a photocopied laugh

Then with a viscose grunt

Wot was hocked and snotted

from the safe black of nothing

into the bleaching light

And the light scorched him clean

Burned the book of him

Baked the mud of love to his docile flesh until it cracked like a mocking smile

And his outsides sang in pain

And his insides trembled with not knowing

Until the furnace of his most middle-middle
coughed a junkyard of words

Each annunciation, a clumsily wielded machete

Hacking at emptiness, like it meant something

And so Wot asked Why?

And was greeted by anemic silence

And so Wot asked, why and why? and why? and why? and WHY? AND
WHY? AND WHY? AND WHY? And so on and so forth

until time and gravity answered
in a language so thick and dense
it bullied him back into the dirt.

Anna Kahn

I Assume You've Heard The Trick to Navigating Possible Hallucinations

which is you take a photo of them and you check
                        if they're in the photo/it would be really quite
                        something to take
                        a photo of a dead girl
                on a bus, no? London packs so thickly
                that it comes down
                to improbable probabilities/take enough
        public transport and *stuff* happens/Rihanna steps on at North Greenwich
                                with four brick shithouses and a tiny man
even more luminous than her/the two people over there
                are the two people your mate cheated on your other mate with
and they don't know you or each other/neither any idea
        their elbow is touching their love affair's
                other love affair's elbow on the Overground/all for you
                        to corner-eye wonder at/the dead
                must get buses
everybody has to get to Whipps Cross somehow/and if
        as the mass of sickly travellers shuffles from the bus stop to the hospital
                                                                itself
you forget   there might be a dead girl three steps behind you
                        that's normal/you've got plenty to worry about
                                without/when she meets
                your eyes in the lift

still and still behind   and is and isn't dead
       and does and doesn't know you
and is and isn't Camila   and you spend three floors of motion not
             knowing
      what is happening or why:
      forgive yourself
for the photo you couldn't take/the ten minutes late you'll be to your
           appointment
     the coping strategies
you absorbed and then ignored/the explanation you will fail to give
      to your flatmate when you come home
         more frightening
      than she has seen you
    so far
your terror/your terror, her face, yes, this is legitimately terrible.

83

Antosh Wojcik

Swimming cures mental illness, said no one, ever, in a doorway, picturing their Dad throwing himself down a staircase

There are brain eating amoeba
in a lake in America,
sometimes America is France,
I swam in a lake in France
in America, there are brain eating
amoeba in a lake in France
in America replaced France,
more brains can be eaten
by amoeba on holiday,
lake-shaped amoeba need vacations too,
said the sabbatical nurse
made from brain matter,
made from France,
she held up Mum's teeth in a jar
and replaced my friend's clothes
with salt, I watched her aftermath
of skin cook in the sun,
hoped she'd climb out of the world,
naked, with me.
The lake in America replaced
the water supply I'm drinking
the lake in France in America,

in the brain eating amoeba,
the size of a bear in my kitchen,
I've had enough thoughts to kill a bear,
once, the amoeba, my brain
undone down to my love,
my love to nothing,
in front of someone
who says I can't be nothing.
I bought a gun made from nothing, once,
an enlarging gun from inside a video game,
for my penis,
shot myself in the face by accident,
mistaking it for my penis,
my head, the size of a bear,
taking me to heaven,
my anatomy's a balloon.
I'm a new people, did-you-hear,
but there are brain eating amoeba
in a lake in heaven.
Ask my brother, in the doorway,
is the holiday ever going to end?
Can I eject myself from the planet?
He's holding a rope, a dumb-pink beam
from inside of the heart
I've been eaten down to,
says he's taking me to swim
in an amoeba, in a brain eating
America that replaced a lake
in heaven, once we leave France.

Salena Godden

not every thing is true

and
all your thoughts
are not facts
you dream
a hundred choices
narrate your life
in a hundred voices
which make you
stop and start
but
not every thing
you think is true
not every think
you thing is true
some of these ideas
they are no good
they are not
magic gold
but jangled bits of
rusty razor songs
and lies that
you stored
and use to
cut yourself
again and again

these fakeries
are buried
in dialogues
you keep like
train tickets
to feeling bad
to teach yourself
a lesson
to remember
to think again
another shit thing again
but not not not
every thing you think
is true
the truth
was a squeaky
squeeze box
nasty noises
so no excuse
so just be quiet
so just be
kind just be as
kind as you can be
because not every
thing you think
is real not every
think you think is real
it's just you feeling
feelings again

and not every
thing
is true
at least be the
best of you
be you
for you
that is the best
you can do
because not every
stinking thinking
dirty shitty thought
you have is real
not every thing
is true
and don't forget
you make stuff up
you do
you really do
and not every
thing is
true

Reuben Woolley

walking dead horses

i & me
        we

go   slow
no go

        the walls of concrete
& wire

        stopped
        zones
we hold in
            handfuls

the sand falls.we don't
                move
dizzy

i & me / we
horizon like
clint eastwood raising dust
killing all
the dirty bastards

            we ask

who writes this
or something else

read me
in
     all
          directions

        i don't move

       the tree

            /

              the five leaves

we've lost our nights

i & me
     we
     go

     bang

Mandy, Beryl, Erica, Jackie,
Lisa, Ange, Edna, Sue, Moira

Salena Godden

When They Took Her Away

When they took her away
she wasn't kicking or screaming.
It was as though
she saw it coming
like she'd been buying time.
I wanted her to shake her fist
tell us she'd show us one day
I thought she'd put up a fight
instead,

when they took her away –
they didn't take her away exactly,
but they led her away –
I saw her lips in a silent whistle
she was exhaling with one breath
she was blowing out a candle
at the end of the night.

As she got into the back seat
they protected her head
she stared, waited patiently
as they secured her seat belt.
She didn't turn
to look at us staring
out the window

but I like to think
I saw the faintest smile
playing in the corner of her mouth
as the car pulled away.

She'll get plenty of bed rest
where she's going
books and telly free hot meals.
It's probably what she needs.
Come to think of it

it's probably what we all need.

Jackie Hagan

Mandy, Beryl, Erica, Jackie, Lisa, Ange, Edna, Sue, Moira

In here everything's broken:
the activity cupboard's broken,
that kettle's broken,
this felt tip's fucked
and I don't know what me hands are for anyway,
just keep banging your head against the wall we know that works.

Come on in,
you might as well,
it's like a holiday from life:
the view
from the dayroom
of men pacing
and holding it in -
til they don't,
women in crazy women coats
with no hope,
sick from trying
and we smoke a lot
and every day at 9 and 12 and 5
for meals we have food
and we smoke our fingers to the bone
and we smoke a lot.

Come on in,
you're just in time -
Beryl's kicking off
screaming awful truths
we all already know
from the last time she kicked off,
with more arms and legs and tears
the nurse's face and blood
and later
she'll come, sedated
into the dayroom,
tail tucked and shamed
that we all know

what we all know

what we all know anyway.

Come on in, it's fuckin great,
it's like an Enid Blyton boarding school,
instead of Matron
we have Elaine the nurse who's overworked and going grey
too early from empathy and no time to care,
Lucy the young nurse on whom it's just dawning
that this system
doesn't work,

but once a week we have ward round!
It's all straighteners and bobbles

and Beth thinks she might get a chance to go home
and Erica's dying
to see her kids,
and we wait

and wait

and wait

until the
LORD OUR SAVIOUR
(the psychiatrist)
is ready
to look at us
in his peripheral vision
with his surprising lack
of
interpersonal skills

considering
he's chosen
to work with
people
and psyches!

You see,
most psychiatrists
need to learn one sentence:
when someone tells you something horrific

that has happened to them
(and they will
because *you* ask them
again and again)
will you just say this please mate:

"I'm really sorry that's happened to you".

David Turner

John Dickson

Raymond throws himself down next to me on the plastic two-seater sofa. With overuse the body of the seat gives, allowing us to slide into its heart. Track-suited thighs touching. As uncomfortable as this is, it is the least of our problems. *How did you sleep Raymond? They tried to fucking poison me again.* I've only been on the ward fifteen days and I've already had enough of Raymond's answer. We sit in purgatory - we've had breakfast and medication but not the morning meeting - the day does not start without the morning meeting. Sit with track-suited thighs touching on plastic cushions watching the same twelve minutes and forty-five seconds of news do endless, patronising forward-rolls on the wide-screen TV (behind scuffed Perspex) on the one wall that isn't covered with A4 sheets offering advice on mindfulness. A4 sheets daubed with spunking cocks, fuck, fuck-off and non-spunking cocks. Lenny screams at Michael. In the twenty minutes since the nurses signed off confirmation that the tablets had been successfully transferred from the McDonalds ketchup pot to Michael's gut he had marched up and down both corridors around twenty-five times. Paul is wanking in the corner. It's still only 8:49. It occurs to me that it's in moments like this that the profound should deliver itself to me. Instead I turn to Raymond and say, *it's alright, Jeremy Kyle'll be on soon.* As poisonous and claustrophobic as it is we rarely look out of the narrow, grated windows. Those locked doors don't keep us in, they keep our ghosts out. I try not to lose my shit over how one newsreader can no longer be trusted to read a story alone. In the courtyard a female patient screams something inaudible in the worst attempt at Jamaican patois prompting Raymond to shout, *that lot downstairs are all fucking mental.* We laugh in unison as the egg-timer is reset.

John Dickson
by David Turner

Nicki Heinen

Solent Ward, Royal Free Hospital, 2008

The nurse says nothing as
he follows me, keeping the length of two corpses
behind me. I see him only out of the corner
of my eye. He comes in to my room
pushes the door behind him, it shuts
with a papery click

Shhh
he says, putting a finger to his lips. He is not much taller
than me, greasy, with a slipped face and stubble
He puts a hand on each of my arms
steadies me in case I run
and leans in, smelling of hand sanitiser. Kisses me
long and hard, making sure I kiss back
He moves his hands to my breasts and feels around slowly
Then he leaves, closing the thin door.

I peel off my gold top and put it in the bin
sit in my bra for a minute. Then I put on a sweatshirt
and retch over the sink
wipe my mouth clean of smeared lipstick
with the blue and white NHS towel, and push open the door.
Walk to the office round the corridor
but he's got there first.

He is talking to a female nurse. She is round
with a silver brooch on her cardigan. Her hair is peppery grey and wispy

I take her out of the room
and tell her what has happened. He is inside typing
a report about me on the desktop computer. I can see my name at the top

She puts on a sympathy face; the corners of her mouth turn down.
I hear her say
Nicki, dear, you're not well.
Nobody here would harm you.
Why don't you go to your room and have a little lie down.

Returning a CD to a Boy Who
is Still Missing

Mona Arshi

Sibling Discount

A phone number
slipped in his hand
outside the supermarket by a

woman wearing ripped jeans
and an REM t-shirt.
Then handwritten messages:

I only flower when
you flower or
Zaungast (and no additional text).

Lucid. Punctual. Relatable.
Two weeks later they were
swapping match cards

whilst the rain rattled on pelting
the tin bowls on his balcony.
By January she had the front door key.

In February she'd removed her
spurs from the sofa stool
given him three cycles of song.

I called for him in Spring but
they said he was already gone.

Dean Atta

No Ascension

You are in hospital, so we buy plane tickets.
You are dying when we reach your bedside.
You are dead, so we wear black for forty days.
Forty days are over but I'm still wearing black.

In London no one knows why.
In Cyprus, we moved as one
black cloud of grief, the whole family
dressed in the same colour

and for once I fitted in with them.
We were all black for forty days.
On the forty-first day my mother says,
We don't have to wear black anymore.

She wears blue jeans and a white top.
I put away my white and all my blues too.
There is only black on my clothes rail.
Casual black, smart black, trendy

East London black, punk black,
sporty black – black is the only colour
I can be, my mother cannot be black with me
and no one else can be black for me.

Either side of your grave I was black.
And this poem is about me, not you.
How I haven't cleaned the mud from your grave
off the shoes I bought for your funeral.

How often I look at the photos I took of you
smiling, dying, dead, and being buried.
How your watch and prayer beads are in the drawer
of this desk I am writing this poem on.

How grief makes much more sense to me
than feeling depressed when times are good.
How a grandfather is meant to die old
and surrounded by his family, just as you did.

How my notebook is a grave and my laptop
is a grave, how my phone is a grave and my bed
is a grave, and there was no ascension after
forty days. And I have stayed buried, with you.

Rachel Long

Beach

In the (third) beginning, I watch the animation, alone.
Impressed, I recommend it to him. He watches the animation.
Then, we arrange a date, meet up, lay down on his blue bed
& watch the animation together.

The animation is about a stick man with a hat, which
he wears to shade his sadness, & contain his brain tumour.
In one scene – a stand-out scene, we agree – he sits, alone
on a beach engraving HELP across the sand. Because
he is an arrangement of sticks, it looks as though he's
using his whole arm. Because he's an arrangement of sticks,
his whole body is a pyre.

At P, he cranes his neck skyward. Or, rather, because he has
no drawn neck, his head rolls back, almost off. Precarious boulder.
Each time he blinks, his eyes become asterisks. It's at this
angle he notices the seagulls eddying & calling to each other: boon,
boon.

Stickman stands. If he had knees they'd be sandy, the land
clinging, *don't go*. He unfolds his arms, juts them out – wings
or crossbar – & runs towards the sea calling, *boon, boon!*

Months later, I'm upstairs doing upstairs things, like brushing
teeth. He, downstairs doing downstairs things, like smashing
a cup, I open my foamy mouth & call, *Boon, Boon! Boon,*
Boon! he calls back without missing a beat.

Now it's all, *Boon, did you remember the dry cleaning?*
Or, *Boon! I swear, you better open this door!*
I first told him I loved him in a hotel room. Plaid sheets.
He sat up, grabbed my hands, blurted it back.
That's it then, I said, *we're fucked.*

Rachel Long

How to Keep Crazy

Never call them Crazy – unless as a compliment,
as in, 'Wow, you're *so* fucked up!' Sleep with them,
even if they won't shower, even if they insist on the dog
gnawing at the foot of the bed. Make jokes
about worse things; War, Tom Cruise, Tories,
Tom Cruise. Fuck at funerals. Do it to the rhythm
of their crying. Peel off each other's black, stare
into his eyes, think sockets, hold him tight, think ribs.
Let him blacken bananas with felt-tip, just unpeel
the knives. Watch a moth headbutt your bedside lamp.
Study it, burning, brain first. Think of the woman
at the shelter who told you all the cats getting run over
recently wasn't the fault of drivers or fast cars, but a rise
in cat suicides. Sometimes he'll panic on perfect days.
Cover him with the tartan scarf. Press a palm to his heart.
Sorry, he says, *my brain*. Learn to sleep with the lights on.
Don't mind that by morning he'll be in the woods. Find him.
Remember to carry a fistful of crumbs for his crows.

Antosh Wojcik

Returning a CD to a Boy Who is Still Missing

My headless body walks to my friend's house,
knocks on his door. Ollie opens.
He is holding a pebble. He asks me to listen to it,
then shows me his art - graphite slashes on paper.
This line is 'sensual'. 'Woman'. This line is 'fear'.
Asked to decipher, I give theories,
low-end interpretations. The wrong answers ping
in his skull. A smile eclipses,
spans ear lobe to ear lobe. Later, his mum
will tell me it was like he had come home.

The doctor covered him in anti-climb paint -
a hand on the shoulder passes right through.
They installed table tennis in his brain,
reinstated him in the family for his parents.
See the serves behind the eyes. No return shot.

Walking home, I pass the play park where the ladders
have been abducted. The kid, who casually decapitated me
with propeller fists, gives me back my head,
like the neighbour re-gifts a football. The kid apologises
for being a helicopter, but I don't blame them,
the brain of play being ladderless.

It's a government scheme, dropping climbable apparatus
into the 'wells of the youth'.
Let's see if they can climb out of themselves.

K-holers line the perimeter of the park - human-shaped
doorways into the ground. I crawl through them
to the whereabouts of whack-a-moles,
to find my gone-friends.
Their faces reappear in the grass wherever I walk.

Antosh Wojcik

The Stoner as Aquanaut

There's a cruelty to a fishhook -
you may damage the mouth
and the catch can die after release.
I can't crack into Ollie
with my hand. I don't trust
these waters of his new habitat,
in the aquanaut suit that has replaced
the ego. At such depths I question
why I want to find him.
Something unfinished from before.
A Q-Tip documentary he'd been making
in his imagination is playing inside
of the helmet, where the face should be.
In a way, he has become the ideal pit,
a blind museum of conquest.
He learned my boyness, balaclava'd
at lunch break
under the Biology staircase. I'm here
for an unmasked 'sorry',
something fathomable,
accepting the blame.

Jack, over beers, says
that was always in him.

Lemon slice dangling like a moon
on the pint surface.
Who's at the bottom of that glass,
looking up,
expecting?

Amy Acre

Maybe

It's Saturday and Dad is naked, sitting in the window
of his and Mum's bedroom, looking out on the front garden,
white Astra, horseshoe viburnum and the crossroads
that regularly brings crash victims to our door
for ambulance calls in a time before mobiles. Dad—briefcase
swinging father of six—is naked, arcing in the window,
one dangling leg like a louche question mark and
he is singing to the blue sky, cock, balls and all.
I am too small to reach the window ledge but big enough
to understand he's not singing because he is happy.

Someone he loves has died, maybe, or he's killing
the shadow of a life my mother lived before they met.
I don't know. I don't know if this incident occurred
before or after the failed suicide attempt Mum will tell me
about two decades after Dad—bearer of business trip t-shirts
slashed with Manhattan's broken half smile—dies of natural causes,
and one decade after my first love follows my first lust
into a nightclub with a knitting needle in his trouser lining
and then deepthroats half a bottle of Co-proxamol.

There is so much I don't know about this window incident,
sometimes I think I made the whole thing up
except I didn't. Except I made up the bit about Saturday.
I don't know what day of the week it is when my father,

who believes in god, is so sad he takes off his clothes
and climbs halfway out of a window, or how many windows
he climbed out of when I wasn't looking, or if people
sometimes remove their clothes when they want to remove
their skin. My dad, who once auditioned for a role in Hair,
has a good voice and when he sings, he can be heard by all
the angels I don't believe in, and the people on the crossroads,
coat-wearing strangers who could die at any moment.

Cecilia Knapp

Mask

I almost didn't notice the mask,
hidden in plain sight, haphazard
dull eyes made of thumb depressions.
Staring out to nothing much.

I see us all in this.
The ways we shrink and hide ourselves.
The many versions we are, twisting into tornado shapes.
Hearts like split lips though we smile hard enough to ignore a purpling
bruise.

I see you.

I am a master at trying to catch your eye,
even though you try with the very bones of you to avoid mine,
you angle your sturdy body away from me and reach
for the jam jar to put your cigarette in.

Grandfathers with blood palms and war stories,
industrial and rough knuckled,
taught you all the ways that you could be a man.
All the ways that you can stay silent.

We wear our own concrete over our skin,
all cement and grit,

we cannot talk to each other so we drink.
I want to open my mouth and swallow your nightmares whole,

I want to talk through the night about your deepest fear
if only you would tell me what it is.

R.A. Villanueva

Albumen

With the name of your first son your mother
speaks of her brothers, stillborn, laid to rest

in the family plot. How the southern
provinces flooded full those seasons, fat

with novenas and rain. We look away.
You kiss his face, open your gown to nurse,

ask for someone to braid your hair. The boy
has lungs like bellows so you make a place

for his lips. Then, there is quiet. We stare
up at the TV, where detectives trawl

a lake front, trace a body with lights, bare
its bruises and cuts. You close your eyes, tell

of his birth in water warm to your waist.
We pray: *Holy Family. O Holy Ghost.*

*

Each of us raised by a family of ghosts
and masks and talking gods. That the Good

Lord knew His mother dreamt nightly of boys

cut down for Him—held their eyes inside
her—is certain. And that we know we have
taken air from those we love is sure. In

albumen prints of Hopi dancers, the
men all have snakes in their hands or teeth, sing
for rain with rattles and whips. Faces flush

with clay or feldspar, the sky behind them
is parchment. They touch feathers to the earth.
Think here of lilies, noise, covenant hymns;

how Palm Sundays we spent the liturgy
knotting crosses from branches, swords from leaves.

*

Not lime or bleach, but oil and spore; knives, sword-
sharp, left to the sink, catching rust. Each day

it proves more difficult to shrug away
the cracks in the moulding, the clots of hair

in the drain. So I say *I love you more
than everything* and mean *You cannot die*

before I do. I mean *Every joy*
we have nests within these bodies' finer

rots. According to the numbers, we don't
have time. Glaciers are losing ground, white smoke

blossoms from a caldera, and your womb
grows tired of waiting for us to talk.

What else do we have? I love you more than
all this. You cannot die before I do.

On Leaving Your Body

Claire Trévien

Brain Fugue

My first fugue was aged 4. My last is yet to come.

- *My brain walked me to our neighbours and asked them to adopt me. My sisters collected me, swore I was fine.*
- *I don't remember my second or third fugue.*
- *The fugues I don't remember are more successful.*
- *I cottoned on that a fugue, to be successful, necessitates a handkerchief tied to a stick.*

A handkerchief cannot hold much on the end of a stick.

- *I walked over the rocks until the sea stopped me, then returned.*
- *Writing adieux can be an effective way to prevent a fugue.*

I accumulated objects for homes I'd never settle in. Then fugued from the boxes.

- *The buildings try to hug me, and I duck out of their arms.*

My relationships became purely digital.

- *My body grew more layers to keep it still.*
- *My brain outgrew the pain in my body. It observed me from the ceiling.*

My in-built satnav tells me when it's time to turn left.

- *Run before they abandon you.*
- *Run before they take your spirit.*
- *Run before the red flags turn bloody.*

Short Film

Sunday, 4am. Woman, 26, drunk, stumbles through her front door, hits light switch with the bulb of her shoulder, waves to the cab driver like he's her oldest, dearest friend. Kicks shoes off. Sighs, grins, performs The Food Dance (shoulders to ears, fists babied, knees bent, sways to broken tune of *Oh, yeah, ooh–oh, yeah*). Walks to bottom of staircase, reaches up, removes battery from fire alarm. She's gonna cook. Oh yeah, she's gonna cook toast. (Drunk woman, 26, hasn't eaten all week, except sweets. Unsure of how to pick this up on camera as she's alone, with no one to tell… Maybe camera can dolly her into the pink-splattered bathroom after? To do: Look into vomit sound effects. Contrastingly, Jazz could play whilst camera waits outside?) Eats/gobbles half a loaf standing up, licks butter and a little of the night's blood off knuckles, left wrist. As she does this, follow her eye-line to the back door, notice her noticing that it is becoming morning. Fiddles with a bunch of back door keys (shows signs of distress at difficulty). It flings open, finally. She's almost in tears (close-up here?). Steps, barefoot, into garden. Floodlit scene. Stray with familiar face walks up steps, she follows its tail past dank pond (would fish floating belly-up be effective here, or too much?), she touches air-raid shelter, lightly, once for good luck (how to communicate this superstition?). Camera locks her in to the middle of abandoned family garden. Removes all her clothes – expressionless – places a tartan scarf over her head; she is going to play 'tents' (childhood game, again, unsure how to get this across. Maybe a flashback scene is needed earlier on – guy's bedroom scene perhaps?). Floodlight times out. Fin.

Amy Acre

Lies you tell yourself and others

And what if you swallow the woods, sell your clothes for a lantern,
lose your name in a city park at night while a security guard
reads *Frutos de Mi Tierra* in the distance.
Far from home's encroaching madness manifest
in the rebellion of lost objects and customer helplines
you root into dense earth, your only route—
to dig yourself out of another woman's body.
Desire is a wicker frame in the shape of a family friend
you burn every sabbath and the grass around your heart
has grown long, obscuring starlings and the grave
of your father. Sick on the local rum, you find
you can lie to your own body and call it adventure.
Like any guilty coloniser, you've fabricated a rootless
accent to render your native English more palatable.

Jasmine Cooray

On Leaving Your Body

The friend's anger crackles like lightning,
Why weren't you there when I needed you?

The speaking and thinking and feeling bits of you
skitter from their homes in your body

like clothes moths evading insecticide
and settle on the ceiling, keeping very still.

The friend's mouth moves, but you only hear
fire, or wind, or water. You try to remember

how to respond, but everything is clunky and out
of time, you are badly dubbed, words crumble

to ash in your mouth. You don't know how long
it will be like this: when you will slip back down

into your body as if it were sand at the bottom
of a slide, but while she is shouting there is this

hammock, this blurry amnion, this cushioned
universe of felt stars, this cool deep ocean.

It is always this way when certain storms come,
when they blow like a storm you remember.

Malaika Kegode

Chips

Our Friday nights always started the same:
fish and chips on Plymouth's Barbican,
that familiar vinegar warmth nestling on our thighs and
legs dangling, spaghetti-like over the water's edge.
We were sixteen, slim-hipped and dangerous,
calling sailors to buy us cider – opaque liquid,
lumps of sour apple floating to the surface,
never fully knowing our power, just knowing
that we loved curry sauce.
Our Friday nights always started the same.

When I was eighteen, my weekdays always
started the same, just as they ended: pinching the swell
of my thighs and hips. Refusing dinner again,
I shrunk myself down to grey 750 calories a day.
One orange for breakfast, one more for tea.
My clavicle was my violin string.
I could never explain why it was so important to be thin,
just knew it was. So it was cigarettes as snacks,
early night gin, papering over the cracks

but I relearned myself through my own history.

When I was six, I always loved how my dad made paratha:
kneading the dough, ghee oozing, sharp and soapy,

layered into flour-dusted surface.
When I was seven, I learnt when food is made together
and the spices are rich, no one could ever make you
feel poor. That week nights should always end the same:
around a table, radiating warmth.

Five years now and my hips are my auntie's hips,
and thighs my own – strong, soft edged.
My weekdays sometimes end the same, though:
pinching the flesh in attempt to tear it off
like hunks of dough in dad's kitchen, eyes prickling
as they did drinking that Sailor cider,
the mother circling the rim...
Happiness is a complicated recipe.

But my Friday nights still end the same:
singing songs of sixpence at 3am,
trotting home clutching familiar vinegar warmth again,
a belly full of fizz and songs.

And whilst hipbones are nice,
I'm starting to think onion rings might be nicer
and I'd love it if you could come round sometime,
so together we can eat chips
and drink some more cider.

R.A. Villanueva

Paternoster

  that night   a wreck   a face   her teeth
beneath a wheel   her dress   your grief

  that night   a field   for deer   a breath
the sound   of bells   a child   to grieve

  a name   a womb   to fill   with glass
and dye   its knots   to test   our grief

  has mass   will bloom   will burn   like gas
will smoke   a harbor   bright with grief

  tonight   a show   for bricks   a tithe
of brass   and dirt   a spine   to grieve

  to run   each street   to church   a raft
of ash   raise high   the beams   for grief

Maria Ferguson

Sleep

Last night I slept in too many clothes.
Layers of cotton, blankets, feathers,
the heaviness forced me to sleep.

Before I close my eyes
I write my dreams.
They're so easy to predict.

I buy clothes that don't fit.
Men's shirts,
oversized dresses,

I drown myself in fabric,
hide my shape, it fluctuates
too often for me to make my peace.

My body pretends to be stable,
it thinks I am stupid.
He used to be more careful

when he touched it.
He used to say my name.
I've started to forget what it sounds like.

How the syllables have
the ability to sink in to skin
and keep you warm.

How back then,
even naked,
I could sleep.

Rebecca Tamás

TIGER

throughout the forest there are big neon signs
the words keep scrambling   or changing
I catch one   then it flicks off to darkness

YOU WERE THE OTHER ONE

FRIENDLESS AND JOYFUL

MADE AND VERY GOOD AT GETTING

close sticking trees
yellow neon then violet

WAITING

why am I in these trees?
I'm not sure I know
is it thick and hot   or cold?
are my footsteps making stupid markings
in the bog or in the snow?

whatever

it will become apparent
because I am not here to inspect myself

I am here   if I am here for anything
for the tiger

when I see the tiger
with rose gold face and expedient teeth
I expect that my life will be changed
I expect that I will understand
I expect that I will undergo total orgasm
I expect that my lips will reach the tiger's face
that I will grow stripes

close trees and closer now
and water making faces at the stars
and trees outline shapes   neat shadow
the water cooling itself
cooling the greened air

my GPS is no longer of use
giving contradictory marks
the tiger could be   anywhere
I could be   anywhere
neon lights   say

FOLLOW

follow   where?

I am so heavy

and   wet and   warm
my bag isn't big   but it weighs on me
thirsty   water in the trees
I don't know which mushrooms   are fine
I just don't know

would a tiger go in a cave?
it smells rich   in there
in there they feed the dead with bread and milk
   get occasional talking therapy
birds screaming outside
I am desperate to be right   and reckless
free   and reckless
complete   and reckless
reckless is a word I will repeat until I am

*

I saw a whale   once
not by looking
but   was   in a boat
and   its enormous   fat glorious mountain self
threw out into air
marked the water   *SLAP   SLAP   SLAP*
marked the air   black   wept crushing
giant slab of wet heat in it   thundering heart
your religion
just looks like shit compared to that   doesn't it?

small open patches here   greenness
one quite large   purple bird   shouting
I call   it   mountain lark
  I give the purple bird my cereal bars

I'm   terribly terribly afraid   it's *great*
they don't tell you how cool it   is
to feel things
skin   prickling   mind prickling
back home   I couldn't see death anywhere
it was   not enough to see a   dead body
I didn't know where the fugue   happened
I wore black   and attempted mourning
but felt entirely   horribly   immortal
   my body   a hot tight insect
circling round   light pathetically

         corpses sit and are sad material
         corpses   sit in thick knowledge
but we   cannot look   inside   them deep   down where it matters

I have sobbed and sobbed   begged
to be a human   creature
   a body not a stone
   a moving spread and not a cavity
  I have begged   to see my place
     blood   and expression
       intelligent questions
          life   like   an   outward   meridian

but death wouldn't come   and debate
 death wouldn't scream at me

death wouldn't shake my   shoulders   wouldn't spit in my face

no matter

the tiger is going to present death to me
on the big platter of its feet

*

the snow is fucking freezing
 and my breaths are tired

perhaps I'll lose weight doing this
which honestly wasn't a consideration
still
if I come back   maybe I can start wearing
ballet cardigans again   in shades of fern green
maybe I can   not get shy   leaning over during sex

in the mirror at home my stomach   is massive
 weirdly fatter than the other 'fat' parts

big square   body mass as if I'm genuinely big
and not kind of   big
not   *big* big
 body   dragging into the pitch   dark road

all my   weird   flesh   not procreating itself
           or   changing   or getting better

I *could* sell the tiger when I find it but I won't
that's complete bullshit
    if I ever   get   out   from   here
             we'll collaborate

the neon signs say:

FOLLOW

THIS COMPLETE AFFLICTION OF HEART MATTER

IS HER LANGUAGE   THE LANGUAGE

I'm going to get eaten
most likely
very likely
I'm pasta
I'm human body   pasta
and I need   to see
that I can die

*

thrumming thrumming
the world is turning itself up to the maximum volume allowed
there are frogs having sex on or near my shoes
covering them in pearly gorgeous slime

apparently spinoza believed that each existent thing   has the capability
of mind
I can feel my insides turning out to look at them
the awful wistful bacteria minds
the smooth beautiful rock minds
the laughing elegant tree minds
the caustic interrupting aroused flower minds
the vibrant shuddering fertile bog minds
the wandering visionary flexible air minds
the interested earnest soil minds
they   touch me in thin and strange places
with creepy   affectionate command

hail comes
with its dark porous communitarian mind
and the rain   with its intelligent desiring witty mind

the hail   is   making me get
beaten up
slapping   down   on my body like it knows me
like it might be able to hurt   open a window   inside

tiger: *come out fucker*

I think it's really rude if he doesn't
because I love him
is someone else   going to even *begin* to
'get him'
in my complete fashion?
is someone   else going to give up everything
they have?

mewling domination   and mutual roaring
he can lie in my lap very still
enormous sexualised cat
with   neon teeth

we can really   make   shame
go   away
we   can   really see living in all the damp red parts
we can really   rush at death   and into it
we can really   bring this sharp joy out   like a wound
releasing   pus

what are those noises?
grand piano   sounds   or recordings
even out here
this might be a death march
   blue fugues
it's way hotter than it should be
isn't it?

I'm sweating
 branches also sweating and slick and black
neon says

AFFIRM IT

SPECTACULAR

CHANGE IN SPACE

I can smell him
I can really smell him
true absolute utter orange
smell of internal organs
smell of   burnt offerings
I can really smell something
like fur and offal!
I can   really smell mud and fire!
I want
I   want   to explode!
I   want   truly   to   exist!

he knows things beyond   these   nothing
of   me he going   in
shadow   all   embraced embraced   embracing embraces
someone film   this   ok

someone   record   how

such   an aesthetic place   such   a

good   selection   of omens

        oh god

he's close   he's close   he's close   he's close he's close he's close

    the fire creeping all   up   fire   cut   and   under   charred   and

mark   his

  his   extreme flammability   extreme

    gap

mind   and

    there he is

there   I   am

Abi Palmer

Dynamite

You are diamonds. Huddled together between layers of dense rock mothers you send out beams. "We are strong," you sparkle. "We are sharp and unbreakable." Positivity radiates through the silent glinting light. *The mothers explode.*

You are back in your childhood bedroom. You are counting sheep. It is late summer and you wonder how you are supposed to sleep when the sun hasn't even gone to bed yet. *The sky explodes.*

You are the manager of a clock shop. A group of studded teenagers have been in, setting all the alarms to go off exactly ten seconds apart from each other. You race round, trying to stop them one by one. The ticking hammers into your head and you think longingly of the bottle of aspirin tucked behind the counter. *A cuckoo clock explodes.*

You are dust. You have been floating through darkness for so long with nothing to cling to. You used to enjoy this but more recently you have thought about settling down, finding yourself a partner. A figure drifts past. In your effort to meet it, you spin a tad too enthusiastically. *You explode.*

You are a brick wall. A man has formed an image of you inside his head. Hoards of telepathic blonde children sit facing him, trying to penetrate your tough and mighty surface. You have been cemented well but the children are starting to dig their minds into all your most vulnerable cracks. *A suitcase explodes.*

You are a lobster. Somebody just tried to dip you into a vat of warm butter, but you have scoured the salty sea bed for eighty years before this and you know when you are being short-changed. *Your claws explode.*

You are a cartoon coyote. You have been attempting to outrun the same meep-meeping bird for so long, but not for the first time, patellar tendonitis is holding you back. You set up a trap. As the bird passes, he steps on a wire, which sets a rock rolling off the edge off a cliff, which lands on a seesaw, which flings a series of darts at a magnifying glass, which is moved into the line of sunshine, which lights the fuse of the largest pile of ACME Corporation™ explosives you can find. You cover your ears and wait for the kaboom. It never comes. You draw your face close to the source of the problem. *It explodes.*

You are a galaxy. You've done pretty well as far as galaxies go. In your early days you were birthing out stars and planets in such abundance that other galaxies drifted into you, sending their asteroid children to encircle your planets in a series of happy moons. But these days you feel old. Your youngest star is flickering and you are not sure you will stand it if another one goes before you. You feel a rupture in your groin.

In Full View of an Audience
the Dreamstage Subject
Sleeps Naturally

Anna Kahn

Notes for Follow-Up with Dr Obasi

- the tin can dawn-lift shake of wake up now
  each eyelash-fight cornea bloodshot sore
- full glass of water heartburn-glugger-down
  with a Rennie's first to peppermint the cure
- mood stabiliser, rails-off-fly-reduce
  (SSRIs were nightmares, never again)
- antipsychotic, not that it's much use
  with the world so fluctuated, norms half bent
- but capable and grateful; every pill
  an NHS prescription-blessing filled

Salena Godden

It's All About the Pathways

K said
we make
neural pathways
in our head
for people
to process ideas
we make connections
and repetitions
K said
grief hurts and
losing someone hurts
and death is painful
because your head
is dissolving
the neural pathway
that was made
for that person
it grows in your head
K said
like a branch of ivy
in your head
K said
and it works the other way
for example
a racist has made a

neural pathway
of hate
a pattern of repetition
a narration of a version
of events
and the more
the racist repeats that story
the thicker that branch grows
when we latch
onto an idea like
loving someone
or like
hating someone
we make a pathway
sticking to one narration
one version about a person or subject
until the ivy knots in our head
K said
and the branch
gets thicker and thicker
the pathways
we create
love and hate
we get stuck
and we
cannot see
reason or light.

Sean Wai Keung

cbt

the challenge of challenging repetitive thoughts
is the feeling of not being in control of those thoughts
+ the challenge of feeling not in control of those thoughts
is the feeling of repetition in the world - in life

like when i was challenged by my therapist to look
back to create a timeline of my cognitive behavioural history
+ i realised then the repetition of my feeling - forever up
down bit further down way up less up down bit
further down down down little up down
up down bit further down way up less
up down down down bit further down way
up less up down bit further down down down little
up down down down up less up down bit further
down + i felt it - that feeling of not being in control
that challenge of feeling that this moment in life
is nothing but another revolution
+ even if it all does ever stop
what would happen next

Sean Wai Keung

i made it

ticking clocks were the worst
all that repetitive clicking
the motion of thought that came
out of it all tick tock tick tock tick
tock kill me kill me kill me kill me
even today i cant stand them
they make me feel like that time
when my therapist mentioned she was
pregnant + i didnt know how to react
+ ive always wanted to write on that
but i dont really know how since a] i dont
know what words i can use to describe
those emotions - like a betrayal kind
of stabbing mixed with a strange
aggressive kind of happiness + also
b] it now sounds like i got my therapist
pregnant which isnt the case at all
much like it wasnt me making
all those clock tick tock kill-mes
+ yet it still felt so personal in the moment
as if i had caused it to be real
which looking back on now
i had

Antosh Wojcik

That time I killed Barney at a barbecue in December

Tuesday is circle time with a group
of fuse-people. See the wicks at the head,
the flame at their gut, close to frag.

I look around the circle, build a hierarchy
of our dooms. A guy gives me his phone number
in case he sleeps for three days straight.
I never call because I forget to ask his name -
and he doesn't turn up the following week
or the week after or the week after.

The floor of the room is made from quicksand.
We have to hit joy before we sink below the surface.

We are taught 'visual-behavioural management techniques' -
Imagine a purple dinosaur and give it your worries to eat.

Naturally, the purple dinosaur is Barney, so in the tunnel
of my body, I'm asking him
where did my happiness go?
and he shrugs,
and ask I him, *how come I have to rely on a purple dinosaur?*
and he shrugs,

we have science guns and the ability to blow holes in the universe
with atoms - casual as toast -
why are you my last resort, Barney?
and he shrugs,
though he doesn't really,
because dinosaurs can't shrug.

Really, Barney, is just an empty costume of a purple dinosaur
draped over a wood chipper. I flush
My American Childhood™ in its teeth –

> [I keep a copy of My American Childhood™
> as another 'visual-behavioural management technique'
> – it looks like a laminate overview of a cartoon town.
> You're supposed to drive cars around, endless.
> No one gets killed because no one
> lives there,
> only empty cars and your hands out the sky]

I realise Barney can't work, so I also put Barney in the woodchipper,
even though he is the woodchipper,
in effect, woodchipping the woodchipper,
and realise too, that the woodchipper
is another 'visual-behavioural management technique'.

This December barbeque is not rational.
Started it to commemorate. Don't bring burgers,
bring your history, quantifiable abandoned objects -
        [ex. the rubber snake from Charlotte

I never liked but took because I thought it was her heart
but it was stupid to visualise a heart
as a gummy lizard where the paint job
was inconsistent.]

They recommend building neutral environments
and sleeping to whale song,
but I still sleep in half a bunk bed -
which is mid-existential crisis itself,
its other half in another room, holding my brother -
where I spent years not sleeping because I thought toothpaste
was going to kill me.

Can you turn the quicksand off, at least? I ask the circle.
They tell me to keep coming back.

This tunnel goes further back than I thought
and I'm here again, echoing into me,
not really knowing what to say.

There's bullshit whale song now, as well.

C.E. Shue

In Full View of an Audience the Dreamstage Subject Sleeps Naturally

Her brain activity displayed on the walls of the exhibit.

They show up in robes, rags, silver sashes, or with muddy feet.

If I say "Red is my favorite color," will you understand what I mean? That red is a lucky color for the Chinese?

Drums made of human bone call the dead, based on the law of similars.

We carry the seeds of conditioning wherever we go; if you mistreat an animal, it becomes afraid.

We become tributaries, basins; we are pools, ponds, streams, and sanctuaries.

But you are not your heart. You are the experiencer of your heart.

Doctrine is meaningless to it.

A different mind is required to receive it.

Tantra means technique.

Whenever the mind says something, think twice.

Fran Lock

the crisis review

stumble-skulled, as usual, the morning makes numb puzzle of a crossword.
fill your name in every blank, for the forty-eight hour crisis review. it would
make a good name for a magazine: *the crisis review.* astounded no one has
thought of it yet. amanda-or-whatever suggests a deeper breath. *i want to be
clean*, i tell her, *fleshless and elect of god.* but up comes everything i'm laden
with, or sodden by. nothing happens right: caffeine's spasm in the hand, my
vehement chemistry, going around challenging chatto poets to a duel. there's
blood on my knuckles again. amanda counts me to ten, but she can't do much
for me. i am inadequately victimised. the light shrinks from the windows, but
people who are *seriously unwell* do not dress in leather and pursue a deviant
ideal in basement bars. i must enact imbalance. over again. such good advice
she's got: going out, taking my corruptible grief for a walk, meeting people,
exercising. *you do want to be well, don't you?* who wouldn't want that?
there's the *miraculous* or the *possible*, and i can't have both. and i can't have
either. and i can't have my cake and hibernate. by which they mean my life.
i tell her *i can feel myself rotting.* she does not find it funny because she
does not get the reference. she doesn't ask me what i'll do when the bad
thought comes, all antique traumas, wasted wishes. she doesn't ask me what
will happen when the genie is out of the bottle: ideation's gremlin, yellow,
poxy, coiled in smoke. what *will* i do? what *will* i get? who knows. leave
the house. early bird gets all the turbulence, a choppy bottled sky round here,
butenal-blue. *you're weird. you're screwed.* interminable dial-tone. a voice
that's going on and on. dogs bark at me as i halt past them, thrusting my
crooked shadow through smoke. and here's the masky face they'd banish
from a library. *i'm not stupid*, i tell her, *i've written books.* but *so much good*

has it done you. in the real world they're paying their bills and mowing their lawns in unison. i've only one thing fit for exploitation: serial abuser, striking his trophy poses. i gave them everything else. but a death is a definite event for amanda. it has a beginning, a middle, and an end, like crummy realist fiction. so, well, fuck this for a game of truth or dare. accentuate extremity with liquid eyeliner. *vulnerable* isn't a word they use about girls from where i'm from. her questions caress me like a bullet with my name on. *have you taken your pill yet today, fran?*

Reuben Woolley

aiming all the questions

with thanks to Jerome Rothenberg

somewhere in here
a stage
& its directions

    i'm looking

lost
  they're
hitting me with
answers.see
the sparks

bright

& my voices have multiplied

     endless

reflect

'It's Alright Ma (I'm Only Bleeding)' / Sorry Fucks

Luke Kennard

One Weird Trick

If I'm distracted it's because
the archive of inconstancy
is being sifted as we speak.
Also that coat looks nice on you.
If angels warn, demons placate,
so all our bad dreams come from God,

But I don't care about that now,
since all advice is bad advice.
If I could be of use to you
I'd wear a mask cut out of cans,
I'd rattle an enchanted staff.

Anxiety isn't cold or hot
nor digital nor analogue;
it takes its cue from Mandelbrot
and Heaven's simple, Hell is not;
what's asked of you is asked a lot
and you will answer as you can.

A colour that you can't perceive,
the surface that you cleaned before,
it's in the timbre of your voice,
a dancing glitch in red on blue.
It's back again. It's back again.

And if the testing of the soul's
grey supermarket's hard to bear,
if the 100 Share Index -
the metaphor that we deserve -
another fetish of the hex…
O satisfy, O amplify.
And if you lose your temper you
can throw a plate into the sink.

A fridge magnet, an office chair,
I'd sooner save your soul than mine.
And that's the cigar guillotine
I mistook for a parlour trick
and chopped my index finger off.
You pointed something out to me.

The angels scowl, the demons cough;
they're always just about to speak,
and you will answer as you can.

Jasmine Cooray

Degrees of Separation

Sometimes I wonder what it would take
to push me from this bit, over here, with clean clothes
and dinner and someone to call—over here
where people sit next to me on the train
and stop me to ask for directions,
where sometimes things are free because you think
I am good and kind, and you don't mind
if I pet your dog, or coo at your baby,

to the other place, where people look away
or stare, then snatch their gaze back
like an animal retreating into a hole
the other place where they whisper together
that poor woman or more likely *I think she's crazy*
and try not to wrinkle their noses at the urine tang
reeking from my dirty jogging bottoms,
and try not to start when my gravel voice shouts

fucker fucking cunt bitch I'll kill you all
because inside my mind is virtual reality
not of now, not even of then, but of some montage
my head patched together from all the bad things
like a quilt of roadkill, like a nightmare on repeat.
And the images mean that I can't see you,
and that means I can't answer questions well
at the job centre, or the doctors, or at school.

I'm not there, I'm here I think as I look
over at the person I could easily be, as I play
with my headphones, look over interview notes.
It's a flimsy assertion. I imagine my internal world
like a jenga tower. Maybe one block is family.
Maybe one block is not growing up hungry and scared.
Maybe one block is being taught to keep my rage in.
Maybe one block is *good girls don't fight, dear.*

Maybe one block is *your body is your own*
Maybe one block is *would you like to be friends?*
Maybe one block is *here is some counselling*
and on and on, the blocks that hold me up:
so that when the rage, the wave that started building
out in the sea of my ancestry, wants to crash in the present
by pushing someone down the escalator
or smashing a pint glass over someone's head

I breathe deeply and cry and call someone,
or maybe I drink and smoke and flirt and talk shit
or maybe I gorge on all the ice-cream in Tesco
but I don't push anyone down the stairs. I stay
on this side, this bit right here, with clean clothes
and dinner, but only because of the set of jenga blocks
I got, which are not the same in every box,
though they'll want you to believe otherwise.

Sean Colletti

On Sleep

You start having nightmares on a
Saturday, which is inconvenient,
because you like things to start on
Sundays. How are you supposed to
respond to your therapist when she
asks, next month, "So, how long have
you been having these nightmares?"
You'll have to say "X number of weeks...
and one day." You grind your teeth.

You come up with stories to tell
your partner to explain why you
wake up screaming: "I had a dream
that I poured a bowl of cereal, but
there was no milk" or "I had a dream
that I was on *Millionaire* and the last
question was about Scandinavian
black metal, so I won, of course" or
"I love you so much, babe, that it
scares me". You grin. She turns over
and covers her ears with a pillow.

You wait until 2:00 a.m. before you
put on a horror film as a form of protest.

If you're going to have nightmares,
you will have them your way, okay?

You feel sleep coming in advance
like a Jehovah's Witness to your door.
You breathe in for three seconds and
hold for three seconds. One: you haven't
taken your socks off yet, but you've
resigned yourself to the fact you won't.
Two: is your heart beating faster than
it should be? Remind yourself to look up
average heart rate tomorrow. Three:
maybe tonight will be different.

You breathe out for three seconds.
Maybe tonight will be different.

Audio   Video

Iris Colomb

I wasn't breathing by myself

Every hour
For the reply
Your decision
My requests

Every hour
I have already
Really concerned with
Your decision

You were expected
You were expected
In your opinion
If it was

Every hour
Really concerned
Already three
For the reply

Every hour
If it was
Every hour
Once or twice

Every hour
My requests.
The only two
Already three

Are you
Are you not
Nothing else
Or are you just

Every hour
The importance of THIS
Is happening here
For the reply

I am guessing
You want to play
You want to play
I need to know

Every hour
The importance
Your decision
Nothing else

Every hour
I am still waiting
Sorry Honey
Guess what

Every hour
You might face
Already three
Previously asked

The last thing I
Can't understand
Or are you just
I need to know

You were expected
I have already
The only two
Enough

Every hour
My requests
The consequences
More than yes

How much you think
How much you think
Or are you just
I need to know

Every hour of THIS
I cannot stress
I cannot stress
Enough

Your opinion
Guess what
I am still waiting
If it was

How much you think
How much you think
How much you think
Is happening here

Every hour
Sorry honey
Every hour
Nothing else

The importance
My requests
Require more
Than yes

Every hour
Your decision
Every hour
If it was

The only two
Already three
I am still waiting
To prove it.

Maria Ferguson

Berocca

I had a dream you were in my parents' old house. The one where I grew up. You were talking to my brother. He liked you. You have never met my brother. He wouldn't like you.

The sun has been shining recently which always makes you feel a bit better, doesn't it? Something about the Vitamin D. Vitamins are good for you. I've been drinking a lot of Berocca lately. It's helping, I think.

It is 3.53pm and I haven't left my bed. Last night I served pints in a pub in East London with two girls I can't stand and a man I'd quite like to sleep with. I drank gin on the sly. Played every trick in the book. Picked up five glasses in each hand at a time, flipped 26 beer mats and shrugged.

When we shut I went across the road to the pub we always slag off and Ethan, a young guy who looked a bit like a skinny Ed Sheeran with glasses, took nearly ten minutes to pour two double gin and slimline tonics and a vodka and diet coke.

My feet stuck to the floor. UK garage vibrated the walls and Ceira and Mel made me laugh and I swayed, shot Disaronno straight and smoked cigarettes, got an Uber home at 2am after escaping a man who said he was lost to which I replied, *aren't we all babe?* before Ceira dragged me away.

My driver was Portuguese. He had a swelling in his cheek, and smelled like cologne and fresh sheets and I ate the dinner I had made but couldn't finish - I can always eat when I'm drunk and I can always sleep but I never remember my dreams.

I keep saying I've been feeling better because the sun's been shining and I've been drinking Berocca but if I'm honest I really don't. So I blame it on the lifestyle - too much to drink, not enough water but we're young aren't we? We're free. This is what we're supposed to be doing.

All my friends are younger than me.
I'm going completely grey.

I keep having dreams about weighing scales, and that old house, and you, and I keep saying I'm going to write.
I keep talking about these great ideas I've done absolutely nothing about

but I've been exercising. I've been moisturising. I've been taking long walks and baths and time, I've been sleeping, I've been taking my time and if you feel so much better, darling, then why don't I feel better too?
If you feel so much better, why am I still drinking Berocca?

Rachel Nwokoro

School Days

under a towering cavernous wreck
i crawled for days in the velveteen deep
fleeing speech

echoing calls of a name i had never had

it could have been 3 miles to the whiteboard
dry wipe my way to the next boulder
that i might lean against

tick tock of the socket

48 times
that's 12 times 4
which
sat right
at the front of the class
seemed as though
maybe i'd pass the Maths exam
and Mum wouldn't crash
head first
into the windscreen
of her jollof-coloured daydreams

if i could sync the tick tock
of the socket
and
the blur of the ball

intercepted
mid
air

                              breeze scraped my knees
                                 and i landed
                         soft cushion of concussion
                                    because no
                            i couldn't make it to
                    the opticians at the back of Boots

                                 not on my own
                             without avoiding lines

                         abacus counting - four times
                                       for my
                   hazy vision and far away glimmers
                                of untainted sight

                         i wouldn't make it back there
            and they wouldn't let me back on the fucking court

                                          since

i held my breath when i crossed the road
or bridges
because legs have a habit of giving way

black and white like zebras
but
mine were viscous cherries
growing across my arm

Roddy Lumsden

'It's Alright Ma (I'm Only Bleeding)' / Sorry Fucks

I am peeing, mid afternoon, just woken, and the blood
drools down my cheek, streaks down my chest. Nothing
explains this. Not a nosebleed. Your blood is pretty much
an old friend you have not seen for a certain-period-agreed.

Head blood. And now I have to mop and staunch, a word
I would avoid at all cost if not needed. But I can make it.
Tamed things swim through the systems of many who dive
behind their kids as if that ushered them to specialness.

Thumbs up people. Sorry fucks who have not casually
bled, almost as habit. Breezers or dullards. All I hope not.
Those who climb behind their shopping, whose hearts
beat weaker to mine. Pleasers, accounted. Life and life only.

My mother phones. Oh, I long to please and in sweet times
can. I am not the robber kitten, the itching pirate, swell
on the gangway of a waning ship. 'Just a nick, Mum'.
She sounds like me. I wipe my cheek through the call.

The razor cut, the eye taken off the onion, handmade blade,
our blood is nearer to us than rats, postage stamps, vans
which are beyond a count. My plan is cautious bleeding.
My plan is to become a land no one can ever settle on.

The Siren Song

Joelle Taylor

Ann Hurley Unscrews a Bottle of Pills

Poor women// we carry our own coffins/ say we don't like flowers/ weave wreathes of lottery tickets and tick books instead/ we build our caskets out of our chip board bed bases/ crowd fund the cremation/ pick the ceremony from a Littlewoods catalogue/ play *Now, That's What I Call Funeral Music*/ to the dearly/ to the gathered/ to the father of the bribed/ to the bitter/ bite the head off the Wake/ awaken in strangers' beds/ a small congregation of pills beside us/ white faces raised in mourning. In revelation.

There is no death. Just less of this. My body is a cemetery anyway.

We say// this is just how she would have wanted it/ no fuss/ eyeing the empty/ the ashtray eyes/ the cigarette spirits/ the street ghosts / we don't look behind us at the deserted pews/ we didn't invite God/ but someone said they saw Him anyway. He should know better than to turn up today. God is a bailiff.

Poor women/ are born into a death/ so soft/ so luxurious/ so fine woven/ that life is almost worth it.

Ann Hurley opens her eyes// lain face up on her childhood bed/ she can hear her mother speaking to food down the stairs/ and the whistle of wide eyes / and it is still dark outside/ as it is this time of year/ but she can smell the beginning of a bird / and the blankets are all she will ever need.

I have never killed a woman who did not deserve it.

Amy León

otra tierra

sin girl
it is to be black
all caught up
all heart attack
a well in your throat
sinking sinking still
relief will come
when the mourning spills

sin girl
it is to be sad
in skin like yours
they will call you mad
consider you sacrifice
consider you dead
take all you are
and call it debt

sin girl
it is to be free
in a world like this
you must bleed
till the siren calls
you out by name
a womb becoming
its own grave

sin girl
sin then call it laughter
swallow the tide
become the water
they will call it drowning
you'll call it birth
dancing in the palm of God
on another earth

Emily Harrison

Slowly Writing My Own Rejection Letter (For The Part of Ophelia)

Darling,
when a woman loses her mind
she gets straight back to
sucking thumbs
demonic stare
stained flowers
on a grimy summer dress
filthy knees and
grubby
grubby
everything

Darling,
when a woman loses her mind
she does not talk about it
she keeps a diary
a lock to be picked with a hair pin
when a woman loses her mind
it is seen and not heard
it is
smiles over teapots
cup and saucer for the teddy bears

When a woman loses her mind
she still giggles
she still hums nursery rhymes
and twirls
and is grateful
when a woman loses her mind
my darling,
she still says
please and thank you

China dolls holding china dolls holding china dolls

Darling,
demure
and deranged
are too close in the dictionary

Gboyega Odubanjo

Grace

I was told that my grandfather liked to travel and that wherever he went he would write his name in big letters into the ground. Last week someone from New Jersey contacted claiming that they had found his name written into one of their ports. There is a general agreement as to the amount of times my grandfather wrote his name into the ground, but nobody can be certain because there are too many ports. My grandfather had seven wives and my grandmother was, amongst other things, my grandfather's first wife. When I ask I am told that she, having failed to predict her own firstness, built herself an anchorite made from her wedding gown and Yoruba words which all translate poorly. When I ask I am told that many of the words that would describe my grandmother translate poorly and so I am told that she was quiet and she died young quietly and that it just happened like that and that there is not really that much to be said about it really.

Malaika Kegode

Bubbles

When the sky begins to change shape
and you learn to stop breathing under water,
perhaps the circumference of thigh you measured
with (limp) pieces of string will seem suddenly irrelevant,
your wrists will stop cracking their stoic melody
and life might seem worth moving for.

Perhaps this will happen.
You will stop walking backwards.

But for now I'm afraid sometimes
it is impossible for life not to seem
retrograded.

Learn to expect the way split lips feel like
rain on a hot day except
everything is under water.
Bubbles.
Fingertip ripples.

Once I watched a documentary on flying fish,
envied their patterns of gliding,
a lesson on how to fit in anywhere…
Stopped trying to fly,
I'm still teaching myself to stop breathing under water.

Being all green and blue and hungry and lonely,
discipline can teach you to wave whilst drowning,
not to swallow the tide or feel reeds between your teeth.
I have always loved the sea.
I believe I always will, even if it envelops me.

Rachel Long

The Yearner

Last night, I stacked three pillows,
made sure my head was heavy with wine, bills,
yesterday's deadline, and I slept hard, tight
as cement on my left arm. The needles came.
At dawn, I dragged it
like a salmon from under my body.
A part of me is dead.
Now I can shake my own hand,
meet myself again for the first time.
How my fingers feel to one another, strangers,
for a tingling moment, I am another.
Promise? My dead right says to my living left,
this time will be different.

Kathryn O'Driscoll

The Siren Song

I've seen light
refracted through the water,
watched the way it bent,
arcing in such balletic beauty before presenting me with something
altogether different from the original.
I've let the tide tell me those tales.
I still believed them anyway.
I've lived in the oil spill of grief for too long.
Settled under the black, with tar-coated optimism
choked down with sertraline, fluoxetine, venlafaxine.

Hope is a fishhook in my throat,
it hurts when I swallow.

I've dislocated my heart and hidden it under the river's tongue,
embedded in a siren song that tries to call me to a home I cannot run
from,
that tells me I belong under the smog of the river.
I've picked the cataracts of depression out of my eyes
and stained my finger-beds trying to scrape them clean.

Through gouged irises I've still seen how clouds,
rolling the day between them like chewed gum,
reflect like evasive promises shivering into smoke when called upon.
I've had my feathers weighted by the sticky-slick cling of memoriam

and merciless self-hatred.
I have found my limbs too heavy to drag them back to safety.
I have drowned
and I have died here.

They found my corpse by the canalside
bloated with the narrative I force-feed myself; that monsters belong
alone,
in swamps,
in agony,
as long as you call it 'home'.
They find me with my tongue swollen out of my mouth
and tell me I can talk to them.
They find me river-wet and wild-hearted,
trying to choke whichever part of me
my head tells me
is trying to suffocate me.

I can't escape this;
I belong in the water. Mermaidic.
All I can do is try to survive a polluted life:
learn how to swim, breathe underwater, and believe
that this is not the blackest hue, this is just a deeper blue
and even the darkest of colour is just light
trying
to be let
back
in.

At A House Party, *Ultralight Beam* Came On & It Started A Church Service

Dean Atta

How to Love Yourself

Write your own list and only take from this
the things that work for you.
Yoga. Running. Walking. Meditation.
A good night's sleep. Drinking plenty of water.
Comfort food. Quality time. Turning off
your phone. Cinema trips alone. Forgiveness.

Do not make a list of your virtues
and vices. Do not do it because of your virtues
or in spite of your vices. Do not feed your fears.
Your fears have an insatiable appetite.
Do not feed your ego. Your ego has an insatiable appetite.
Learn to live with a certain amount of hunger.

Do not expect to be full all of the time.
Do not place parts of yourself on the table to be dined upon.
Go to the library and take yourself off the shelf.
Check yourself out. Read yourself.
If you are not satisfied with how your story reads,
make as many edits as you want to.

Take the new edition of yourself back to the library
and if asked about the edits, politely, or not
so politely, remind them that you are the author.
When no one turns up to your poetry reading,

read the poems out loud anyway. When no one turns up
to be your father, grow up to become a great man anyway.

Say your name out loud until you feel good
about the way it sounds. If that proves impossible
– rename yourself. Remember
if you rename yourself for a laugh
too many times on Facebook, you may get stuck
with a bad joke. Learn to laugh at yourself more often.

Do not spend too much time on social media
looking at other people's photos, relationships,
marriages or Valentines. Refuse
to acknowledge February 14th as any more important
than any other day. Do not compare
your days to anyone else's.

Yes, you have the same amount of hours
in the day as Beyoncé but you are not Beyoncé.
Find yourself. Find yourself attractive.
If that proves impossible – relearn what attractive is.
You are not tinder, you are already flame.
Swipe right to your reflection every morning.

Say this in the mirror, "I accept myself
unconditionally right now." Remember
that just because someone is single and finds you
attractive and good company
that does not mean they will be able to love you.
There are many reasons someone may not

be able to love you that are not about you.
Their reasons are not your faults, not your reflection.
Their reasons belong to them.
Remember that no one belongs to you, but you.
No one knows you as well as you do
and your list needn't read anything like this.

Joelle Taylor

in this poem i am a time traveller

for my mother

may it reach you bovine in the shower, that
morning, erased by water,
as you decorate bridal white tile with red confetti, his
shadow unlearning itself on the way to work;
may it stop at the cubicle door for a moment
and recognise its own father's face
in the embryos of air. may it smile once, and feel guilty.
may it walk right out of the house
a pause to throw a kiss
like a grenade at the blonde haired boy
who never learned to navigate
            the tight corners of his mouth
who slipped and fell years ago
                may it slam the fucking door
like last year,
may it walk forward   and onward   still
past the man with the face of zeroes, the young girl threading dogshit
hearts together
on newspaper string. may it stop by the busker
and whisper the next words, may it bring
unaccountable melody, an orchestra of ancestors humming,
may it run for the bus   for a bus that is always running
may it stay a while with the driver
whose eyes are Arab Spring, who is hard, is cliff, and

know this brick wall
surrounds a garden,
may it comfort his angry and his small, may
it rock him rock him rock
may it go straight to the top deck of the bus
smack foot and riot smell
may it yell discordant sonatas   something strange   something wrong   at the
film reel unravelling outside
may it see your face. your sudden face.
crowded there with crossings out
may it read. may it lean closer. may it read.
may it sit beside you
for just this once
just this journey
may it hold your hand,
and you remember child
may it cradle your palm
like a woman rescued
like in that story of the
small girl
who ate herself,
and became
everything else.

May you be loved. May you feel it. May you wear it today instead of that
bright dress. Instead, of him.

Gabriel Jones

How to let go of the Moon.

(i)

The moon doesn't exist, snarls John, well, not like *that*
stop twisting my words! and stop philosophizing, the colour -
he says - is *parlour dove off-white*, Screwfix do cans for 3.99.

He's been practising the exact brushstrokes for a waxing crescent
holding ruler index against cloudless nights, mouthing
centre to perimeter. pirsquared-PI-R-squared. I catch tears

streaming into his pint. It's the moon that controls the saline sea
I offer (half rudimentary handkerchief half dig-in-the-ribs)
we must have looked in wonder for years. My mum says

you dream more when it's full. He say come on now, stop being
obsessive, there's onions cooking, Zayn Malik just had a break up,
morning drizzle, sweat, the news, there's a million reasons. Don't be soft.

(ii)

I remember a half year spent inside ruining my parents furniture,
painting off-white circles on the backs of chairs and walls, trying
to dive into the glowing targets, banging my head and swearing.

I remember stretching out both arms, tiptoeing right foot on America,
left in the Atlantic, pulling against orbit, prizing moon from hanging,
just about getting lips around and swallowing the swollen fruit.

Un-chewed, it golf-balled my oesophagus and I preened
to show how close it sat to my heart and bumped into bush.
I have a best friend now, who can say from the temporary dark

You've gobbled the moon again, fatty, you're burping bits of rock
and I know to reach into myself, take a gentle fist around the moon
hold my arm above my head and open my palm.

Caleb Femi

At A House Party, *Ultralight Beam* Came On & It Started A Church Service

and in the corner,
two spiders watched
us tranced by the words of
the little girl pouring through
the speakers like anointing oil

    we don't want no devils in the house

and one spider said to the other,
this is how they exalt so be careful,
they'll not notice treading on you
and the other spider said yes
we are watching our devils
pray away their devils.

    when they come for you, I will shield your name

The bass made your eyes heavy
like that time with the mandem
in a Vauxhall ringer, hotboxing
trying to come up with a name
the streets will know you all by.

    deliver us peace. deliver us loving

Things with names deserve deliverance,
that's why you don't name the spiders
you find scuttering across your kitchen floor
otherwise your house will become a sanctuary.

Father this prayer is for everyone that feels they're not good enough

The name given to you by your father is not your real name,
it is your occupation in this world, determines
how many friends you will have,
how many of your CVs will be discarded without even a glance,
how much Justice you will be afforded,
how many lovers will think twice about introducing you to family,
how much money you will make, ever.

this is a God dream

Did you know that God takes down the names
of everyone who pays their tithe,
everyone who says His name in vain,
that there is a book with all
the names of everyone who will see Heaven.

Jolade Olusanya

still shines:

young man,
the sun still shines.

remember this:
at your lowest
at your darkest

when doubt hangs from your heart like a wet jumper on a wire hanger
tugging all in the hopes that a warmth will dry your body of its dampness

the sun still shines young man.

even beyond the grey clouds of your self-esteem.
beyond the absence of physical warmth.
beyond all.

before you and after,
it still shines young man.

the sun still shines.

Deanna Rodger

Things I learnt today

Getting out of the house is fine
Even if you didn't tell the person who forced you out, where or when to
meet and they are in a onesie and will be for another hour.
You don't have to drive
Taking your time usually means that the train will arrive on time
Browsing doesn't need to be disturbed
Politics in front of customers is not the one
What was what you assumed isn't always is
Buses sometimes have to be walked for
These too will arrive without you having to run
Home always remembers to bring her keys
Front rooms are the comfort you want
Tasks are better done with a smile
Your sister is your best friend
Working with your best friend can be the last thing you need
Parks were made to cry in
Mud is softer
Narrow streets have big houses
Some drivers also climb out of the passenger seats
Your old school uniform is a source of pride
Fancy cars get scratched too
Charity shops hold the word cunt
Nomad books shelter mums
The work has begun
Daughters fly away

Distraction is food
Urban Buddhas give free advice
Peace is in the childhood library
Phones make you early
Buses don't always come quickly
There is no rush
Meetings deserve hot chocolate
Fulham Broadway is home
Blue haired women forget you know the trains
You don't mind
Rediscovering yourself is important
Seats should been given to the pointers
Hips aren't broken
Double stepping the escalator gets you halfway
Some people are alone
Nhs staff deal with their shit
Physio is an opportunity to show off
Resolution
Lifts lack reception
Euston reminds you not to run
Big mouthed women are attractive
Old street is red
Old street is more than the roundabout
Standing still at a junction is calming
Friends are where they want to be
Eye patches form communities
Comedy is dedication
Watching stuff is work
Non monogamy has an event
I know what's this is

Death club exists
Nights have their own life
Starting is a rhetorical question
Tea accompanies great poetry brilliantly
Questions are important
Three is enough
Family take up space
They dig for truth
Best mates don't need to be sat next to
Waking up is success
Circles don't hold their shape in the smoke
Choice is quicker
Running is a six min wait
Coins can be flipped on empty carriages
Passengers manage each other
Exes waft in scents
Unsullied love smells great
Metro star signs aren't as true read at the end of the day
No matter how much you do
This list is incomplete

Rachel Nwokoro

Expectations

i pity all of those versions of me
frozen by the belief that they
should
be
doing
better

you are here little one

the universe expects nothing from you
your birth and your death are inevitable

to live is the choice

Rob Auton

Why Yellow?

Yellow because I don't want to live my life in the dark
I don't want to live in the shadow of my death
I want to live on the bright side
ON FULL BEAM WITH CAPS LOCK ON
I want to stand and to stand for standing up
To try to do good and to be a good person
To shine away from politics and war
and all the other important things I don't understand
That I know for a fact we as a species have made up
Someone drew the letter O for the first time
It just caught on and it wasn't that long ago
I look at politicians and cannot relate to them in any way
I know they have faces and hands and fingers with fingernails
I know that they need to eat and to sleep and to feed their families
Sometimes it feels like the world is a pub quiz and I am sat at a table on
my own and I don't know any of the answers
But I look to the sun and feel the warmth on my face and am certain that
this is something real that humans have always done and always will do
no matter how absurd this planet gets
Yellow hope
Yellow to me is the light that isn't at the end of the tunnel
It's the light that surrounds us
It's a poached or boiled or scrambled or fried egg on a Saturday morning
If that egg was grey instead of yellow

Would the experience be as magical?
Grey scrambled egg served on a bed of death
That's what I'm fighting against

Dizraeli

Everybody here's golden

Note: The lyrics to this song were actually written in December, although to me they feel like the spring. After a long dark patch, there was a day when I woke up and there seemed to be a different quality to everything, suddenly there was air and space around things, and I could forgive and be forgiven. It was an indescribable feeling but here's an attempt to describe it.

"I don't walk
I get carried"
           - Ol' Dirty Bastard

Sleepless
Damp twisted sheets
Angular as a word of a lie
I fling up window and out there is
Open throated engines
and a bird of a sky
Timothy slides into quicksand
Good riddance to his murderer's eyes
A gurgle and he's gone
It's just me and the garden
Screaming as it bursts into light
Who am I to try and drown it out?
In the urban decline I clock
Finsbury Park with its crown of clouds

Beatific smiles on the down and outs
Buzzed from the first hit of the day
I clock
Buff roofers in the altogether
I clock
A buck toothed lady with a sticky out belly
Preggers belly button like a cherry on the top

And everybody here's golden
Everybody here's golden
Hear the sun stream in
Everybody here's golden
Everybody here's golden
See the sun stream in

I think of her and I think of her
Til ambulances are a distant murmur
I turn left towards Rich Mix
Hipster district
I'm switching off my inner judge
I see a man with a gun
in Kevlar, black boots and these dreamy eyes
Like he's thinking of his lover too
Thinking we should have a baby
Thinking
          she's so nice
And people drink tequila do the twist
And I forgive them all for everything
Seeking pleasure for their penises or mouths
Futureless

Trying to shake the sediment
In the gathering catastrophe
Calm is a super power
I switch mine on
And whatever happens
we are family
and I have reached the venue
and we will be fine hun..

And everybody here's golden
Everybody here's golden
Hear the sun stream in
Everybody here's golden
Everybody here's golden
See the sun stream in

Acknowledgements

'How to Love Yourself' and 'How to Say Goodbye' by Dean Atta were published in *Important Nothings — Creative Future Literary Award Winners*, and 'How to Love Yourself' was first aired on BBC World Service. 'No Ascension' was first published in *Going Down Swinging #38* and shortlisted for the Out-Spoken Prize for Poetry 2018.

'Men Locked Behind Toilet Doors' was previously published in the Flapjack Press book *No Tigers*, the third single author collection of poetry by Dominic Berry.

'Dragon Hill Spa' by Mary Jean Chan was first published in *The Rialto* and 'Rise and Shine' was published in her debut pamphlet *A Hurry of English* (ignitionpress, 2018).

'Everybody here's golden' appears on Dizraeli's forthcoming album, *The Unmaster*.

'It's All About the Pathways' by Salena Godden is published in *Pessimism is for Lightweights* (Rough Trade Books, 2018). 'When They Took Her Away' appeared in her pamphlet, *Under the Pier* (Nasty Little Press, 2011).

'Mandy, Beryl, Erica, Jackie, Lisa, Ange, Edna, Sue, Moira' was published in *Asylum* magazine and appears in *Some People Have Too Many Legs* by Jackie Hagan, (Flapjack Press, 2015).

'Solent Ward, Royal Free Hospital, 2008' by Nicki Heinen was first published in her pamphlet, *Itch* (Eyewear Press, 2017).

'How to let go of the Moon.' by Gabriel Jones was first published in the 2017 Barbican Young Poets anthology, *An Orchestra of Feathers and Bone*.

'Heroin' by Melissa-Lee Houghton was previously published in *The Scores*.

'a backward dark' by Fran Lock appeared on the *Culture Matters* website.

'The Yearner' by Rachel Long was published in *Ash*, University of Oxford Poetry Society magazine, February 2018.

'"It's Alright Ma (I'm Only Bleeding)" / Sorry Fucks' and 'Written While Weepy' by Roddy Lumsden appear in the forthcoming *Blue of Noon* anthology.

An earlier version of 'In Full View of an Audience the Dreamstage Subject Sleeps Naturally' by C.E. Shue was published in *Drunken Boat*, Issue 16, October 2012.

'Quiet Places' by Lemn Sissay was published in his collection, *Morning Breaks in the Elevator* (Payback Press, an imprint of Canongate Books, 1999).

'Albumen' by R.A. Villanueva first appeared in *The Common*. 'Paternoster' first appeared in *Poems in Which*, and 'Saudade' in *Prac Crit*.

~

We owe a huge debt of gratitude to Arts Council England, for giving us the financial support that made this book possible. In this regard, we are also massively grateful to Liz Counsell, whose kind and constructive advice helped us to secure this funding.

We are in awe of the design talents of Lynne Eve, who created the cover of the book, and grateful for the time and craft that she put into the project.

Thanks also to Anne Macaulay for her eagle-eyed proofreading.

Thanks to Tyrone Lewis and Process Productions, who filmed and edited video versions of some of these poems; and to David Turner, who kindly recorded audio. We also owe thanks to Raise the Bar, for allowing us to link to their video of 'Men Locked Behind Toilet Doors' by Dominic Berry, and Tate Britain, for the film of 'Mask' by Cecilia Knapp.

To Malika Kegode at Milk Poetry, Sean Colletti, Stuart Bartholomew at Verve Poetry, and Henry Raby at Say Owt, for their partnership in running the book's launch events; and to Rich Mix in London, Wardrobe Theatre in Bristol, Waterstones Birmingham and All Saints Church in York.

A large body of work about mental health, while hugely rewarding to put together, can be a tricky thing to be with day after day. We'd like to thank our friends and family for supporting and distracting us; in particular, our parents, Gill, Amy and Alex; and our children, Solomon and Billie.

Finally, we'd like to thank every caregiver, nurse, doctor, therapist, NHS staff member, medical professional, friend or stranger who has come to the aid of any of the people in this book, in a time of need. The miracles you perform every day are a far greater achievement than any book.

About the Authors

Amy Acre is a poet, performer and freelance writer from London, and the editor of Bad Betty Press. Her pamphlet, *Where We're Going, We Don't Need Roads* (flipped eye, 2015) was chosen as a PBS Pamphlet Choice and a Poetry School Best Book.

Raymond Antrobus is a Hackney born British Jamaican poet, educator, editor and curator of Chill Pill. *To Sweeten Bitter* (2017) is published by Out-Spoken Press and his forth-coming debut, *The Perseverance* (2018) is published by Penned In The Margins.

Mona Arshi lives in London. Her debut collection *Small Hands* was published by Pavilion Poetry, part of Liverpool University Press and won the Forward Prize for best first collection in 2015. Her second collection will be published in Spring 2019.

Dean Atta was named one of the most influential LGBT people in the UK by the Independent on Sunday Pink List, and has performed widely across the UK and internationally. He's been commissioned by BBC Radio 4, BBC World Service, Dazed & Confused, Keats House Museum, National Portrait Gallery, Tate Britain and Tate Modern. His debut collection, *I Am Nobody's Nigger*, was shortlisted for the Polari First Book Prize. He co-produces spoken word night Come Rhyme With Me alongside Deanna Rodger, and is Guest Artistic Director of New Writing South.

Joel Auterson is a poet from Belfast, living in London. He co-hosts Boomerang Club, one of London's best-loved poetry nights, now in its fourth year. He's performed around the UK and at festivals like Bestival,

Nozstock and the Edinburgh Fringe. He was part of the Roundhouse Poetry Collective in 2014, and was a resident artist at the Roundhouse for two years. His first book, *Unremember*, was published in 2017.

Rob Auton was born in Yorkshire in the early nineteen eighties. He is a writer and performer of some of what he writes.

Dominic Berry was 2017 Glastonbury Festival Poet in Residence, and winner of the 2017 Saboteur Award for Best Spoken Word Artist. His most recent poetry collection, *No Tigers*, is available through Flapjack Press.

Mary Jean Chan was shortlisted for the 2017 Forward Prize for Best Single Poem. Her debut pamphlet is out with ignitionpress (2018), with her debut collection forthcoming from Faber & Faber in July 2019.

Sean Colletti was born and raised in California. He came to the UK to pursue education and writing, getting his MA in Creative Writing: Prose at the University of East Anglia, and he is in the final year of his PhD at the University of Birmingham. He has headlined at spoken word nights across the country and was part of the winning slam team at UniSlam 2018. His first pamphlet, published by Bare Fiction, is due in autumn 2018.

Iris Colomb is a poet, artist, translator and curator based in London. She has been resident artist and poet at the Centre For Recent Drawing; she is the art Editor of Haverthorn magazine, and a member of the interdisciplinary collective, No Such Thing. Her work has been exhibited at the National Poetry Library, and her co-translation (with Elliot Koubis) of *The Stories and Adventures of the Baron d'Ormesan*, a series of short stories by Guillaume Apollinaire, was published in 2017.

Jasmine Ann Cooray is a poet, facilitator and counsellor from London, of Sri Lankan and mixed European lineage. She teaches others to use creative tools to access humanity and joy. Her abstract accolades include: 2013 Writer in Residence at the National University of Singapore, a 2015 BBC Performing Arts Fellow, a 2017 Spread the Word Associate Writer. To balance her reclusiveness, she does an excellent line in hugs.

Dizraeli is a poet, producer, MC and multi-instrumentalist, pushing the boundaries of hiphop, drawing on grime, jazz, garage and West African percussion to craft a genre all his own. He's supported Saul Williams and Mos Def on their UK tours, worked with Kate Tempest and Scroobius Pip and had his music played on BBC Radio 1, 1Xtra, Radio 2, Radio 3 and 6Music. In 2018 he's back with *The Unmaster*, his first self-produced album.

Caleb Femi is poet hailing from south London. He is featured in the Dazed 100 list of the next generation shaping youth culture. Using film, photography and music, he is passionate about pushing the boundaries of poetry both on the page, in performance and on digital mediums. Caleb was the first Young People's Laureate for London.

Maria Ferguson is a writer and performer from Essex. She has performed extensively across the UK as well as at festivals such as Bestival, Latitude and Secret Garden Party. She has been commissioned by Roundhouse, The Royal Academy of Art and BBC Radio One. Her debut show *Fat Girls Don't Dance*, is published by Oberon Books and won the Saboteur Award for Best Spoken Word Show, 2017. She is currently working on her second show, *Essex Girl*.

Kat François is a performance artist, broadcaster, playwright and director. *Raising Lazarus*, her play dealing with the experiences of Caribbean soldiers in World War One, continues to tour globally to critical acclaim as part of the WW1 centenary and featured at Imperial War Museum. Kat has worked with young people for many years as a youth worker, PSHE Facilitator, teaching dance, drama, poetry and performance skills.

Anne Gill is studying for a masters in poetry at Newcastle University. She was part of the University of Birmingham's slam team, winning Unislam 2018 and competing at CUPSI in the US. She has performed at events across the UK and was shortlisted for the Out-Spoken Prize for Poetry in 2018. If you talk to her she will probably tell that she loves cats.

Salena Godden is one of Britain's foremost poets; author of *Under The Pier* (Nasty Little Press), *Fishing in the Aftermath: Poems 1994–2014* (Burning Eye), literary memoir *Springfield Road* (Unbound) and 'Shade' published in the groundbreaking anthology *The Good Immigrant* (Unbound). Her poetry album *LIVEwire* was shortlisted for the Ted Hughes Award in 2017. *Pessimism Is For Lightweights*, 13 pieces of courage and resistance, will be published by Rough Trade Books in June 2018.

Jackie Hagan is a multi award winning playwright, poet, writer and performer who has delivered over a thousand workshops in prisons, secure psychiatric units, pubs and schools. She is a working class, queer amputee from Skem and champions the vilified, forgotten and failed.

Jake Wild Hall is one half of Bad Betty Press, the host of Boomerang Club and PBH's 2016 Spirit Of The Free Fringe. His debut pamphlet *Solomon's World* was longlisted for Best Pamphlet in the 2018 Saboteur Awards. He really likes cheese and peanut butter together.

Emily Harrison performs regularly in London and across the UK. Winning Best Spoken Word Performer at the Saboteur Awards, Emily continues to be encouraged by audiences and NHS professionals to give a room full of strangers questionable advice on how to live your best life in and out of the psychiatric institution. Her first full-length collection *I Can't Sleep 'cause My Bed's On Fire* was released with Burning Eye Books in 2016.

Nicki Heinen studied English at Girton College, Cambridge University, where she won the Barbara Wrigley Prize for Poetry. Her work has been published in magazines and anthologies including Magma, Holdfast, Rising, and Tentacular, and was shortlisted for the Pat Kavanagh Prize in 2012. She founded and hosts Words & Jazz, a spoken word and music night, at the Vortex Jazz Café, London. Her pamphlet *Itch* was launched with Eyewear Press in May 2017. She lives in North London.

Gabriel Jones is a poet, spoken word artist and music producer, blending everyday and surreal narratives set between Wales and London. He has performed his work across the UK including at Bestival, Roundhouse, Bradford literature festival, FTRW and Lovebox. He is a Barbican Young Poets alumnus and is currently putting soundscapes and beats to some of the most exciting voices in poetry.

Anna Kahn is the host of the Unfinished Edits podcast. She's a Barbican Young Poet and a former member of the Roundhouse Collective. Her work has been published by *The London Magazine*, *Right Hand Pointing* and *The Rialto*, amongst others.

Malaika Kegode is a poet, performer and promoter from the South West. She has worked closely with Apples and Snakes to host Spokes Amaze, and her own event Milk Poetry has been a well-received addition to the Bristol poetry scene. She has performed at Bristol Old Vic, Boomtown Festival, Tobacco Factory Theatre and Hammer & Tongue and worked with organisations such as BBC 1Xtra and the Roundhouse.

Luke Kennard is a poet and novelist who lives in Birmingham. His most recent collection of poems, *Cain* (Penned in the Margins, 2016) was shortlisted for the International Dylan Thomas Prize and his first novel, *The Transition*, was published by 4th Estate in 2017.

Sean Wai Keung suffered a period of mental illness in his late teens, making it through thanks to tireless support from various NHS mental health professionals and groups. He went on to attend Roehampton University and the University of East Anglia, after which his debut poetry pamphlet *you are mistaken* won the inaugural Rialto Open Pamphlet Competition. He has worked with the National Theatre of Scotland, National Library of Scotland, Apples & Snakes and Speculative Books among others.

Cecilia Knapp is a poet, writer and theatre maker. Her commissions have included the TATE and the BBC, and she has been featured on BBC Radio 1 and Channel 4 as well as in *Vogue*. Her debut collection will be released in November 2018 and she is working on her first novel.

Melissa Lee-Houghton was born in 1982. Her most recent collection, *Sunshine* (Penned In The Margins, 2016) was shortlisted for the Ted Hughes Award, The Costa Book Award and the Forward Prize, and won a Somerset Maugham Award. In 2015, *The Faithful Look Away* won her a Northern Writers' Award, and she has broadcast two of her short stories on BBC Radio Four. She is a Next Generation Poet.

Amy León is a musician, poet and educator. She performs frequently all over New York and has toured the UK numerous times, performing in collaboration with the BBC, Roundhouse and Amnesty International. An alumna of the Nuyorican Slam Team, her work focuses on social inequalities, celebrating love, blackness and what it means to be woman. She is the author of poetry collections, *the water under the bridge* and *Mouth Full of Concrete*. Her debut album *Something Melancholy* is available now.

Fran Lock is the author of four books, *Flatrock* (Little Episodes, 2011), *The Mystic and the Pig Thief* (Salt, 2014), *Dogtooth* (Out-Spoken Press, 2017) and *Muses & Bruises* (Manifesto Press, 2017). She is currently struggling through an ill-advised PhD at Birkbeck on the relationship between the epistolary form in contemporary poetry and the use of letters in therapeutic contexts.

Rachel Long is a poet and the founder of Octavia - Poetry Collective for Womxn of Colour, which is housed at Southbank Centre, London. She is Assistant Tutor to Jacob Sam-La Rose on the Barbican Young Poets programme 2015-present.

Roddy Lumsden has published seven collections of poetry, several chapbooks and collections of trivia, and edited several anthologies. His first book, *Yeah Yeah Yeah* (Bloodaxe, 1997), was shortlisted for a Forward Prize. His second, *The Book of Love* (2000), and most recent, *So Glad I'm Me* (2017) were shortlisted for the T.S. Eliot Prize. He's edited several prize-winning poetry collections, the Pilot series of chapbooks for Tall Lighthouse, and between 2010 and 2013, was Poetry Editor for Salt Publishing.

Katie Metcalfe is a more-Scandinavian-than-she-is-English writer, blogger, poet and publisher. She's also a new mum, a proud weirdo and an introvert living with bi-polar. She's published several collections of poetry including: *Dying Is Forbidden In Longyearbyen, In The Hours Of Darkness* and *My Father The Wendigo.*

Rachel Nwokoro is a writer, actor, spoken word artist and mental health vlogger of Nigerian heritage, born and bred in London. Unapologetic in communication, she enjoys finding beauty in dark spaces, and is dedicated to diversifying the representation of minorities in the performance industry. In 2016 she was the UK SLAM Champion, a World SLAM Championship Semi-Finalist and Roundhouse SLAM Finalist. Her first collection is out with Burning Eye Books in 2019.

Kathryn O'Driscoll is a disabled slam winning poet from the South West who focuses heavily on mental health experience, LGBTQ+ issues and loss.

Gboyega Odubanjo is a British-Nigerian poet, born and raised in East London. He is currently studying for an MA in Poetry at the University of East Anglia. His debut pamphlet will be out with Bad Betty Press in 2019.

Jolade Olusanya is a Nigerian poet, director and photographer based in East London. He is a Barbican Young Poet, board member of literary organization Writerz n Scribez and member of multi-disciplinary creative collective SXWKS. He's currently working on new poetry films and his debut poetry collection. In 2017, he was awarded the Out-Spoken Prize for Performance Poetry and the overall Out-Spoken Prize for Poetry 2017.

Abi Palmer is an interactive writer and artist. Her current project, 'Sanatorium', funded by Arts Council England, explores the relationship between language, movement, and the body. Her essay 'No Body to Write With: Intrusion as a Manifesto for D/deaf and Disabled Writers' was published in *Stairs and Whispers: D/deaf and Disabled Poets Write Back*

(Nine Arches Press, 2017). Her multisensory poetry installation 'Alchemy' was awarded Best Wildcard at the Saboteur Literary Awards 2016.

Bobby Parker was born in 1982 and lives in Kidderminster. His publications include the critically acclaimed *Ghost Town Music* and *Comberton*, both published by Knives Forks & Spoons Press. Nine Arches Press published his first full-length collection of poetry, *Blue Movie*, on Halloween 2014. He has written articles on poetry for *The Quietus*, and tours the UK promoting his books and mental health awareness. His new collection, *Working Class Voodoo*, is out now with Offord Road Books.

Deanna Rodger is an international writer, performer and facilitator. She co-curates Chill Pill and Come Rhyme With Me, and is on the board of Safe Ground. Commissions include Under The Skin (St Paul's Cathedral), Now We Are Here (Young Vic), Women Who Spit (BBC iPlayer) and Buckingham Palace (NYT). Accolades include ELLE UK's '30 inspirational women under 30', The Female Lead's '20intheir20s', Cosmopolitan's 'No.1 trailblazing woman', and youngest UK Poetry Slam Champion (2007/8). She teaches Writing Poetry for Performance with Benjamin Zephaniah at Brunel University and is a tutor at School of Communication Arts. Currently in development with EARTH: The Show.

C.E. Shue earned an MFA in Poetry from the University of San Francisco. Her work has appeared in *Entropy, Versal, Washington Square, The Collagist, sparkle + blink, Works & Days Quarterly, Storyscape* and *New Flash Fiction Review*. A Kundiman Fellow, she has received support from the Vermont Studio Center, the Provincetown Fine Arts Center, and the University of San Francisco. Her photography and poetry featured in the 92nd Street Y's #wordswelivein project and she has collaborated on a musical poem, 'Lucid: Dream For' for composer Jerry Gerber's CD, Virtual Harmonics.

Lemn Sissay MBE is author of a series of books of poetry alongside articles, records, broadcasts, public art, commissions and plays. Lemn was the first poet commissioned to write for London Olympics. His Landmark Poems are installed throughout Manchester and London. They can be seen in The Royal Festival Hall and The Olympic Park. Lemn was official poet for The FA Cup 2015 and his Desert Island Discs was pick of the year for BBC Radio 4 2015. Lemn is Chancellor of The University of Manchester, Patron of The Letterbox Club, Canterbury's Poet Laureate and he is a regular contributor to radio and television.

Ruth Sutoyé is a poet, facilitator, creative producer and visual artist. She is a Barbican Young Poet alumna and member of the SXWKS collective. Her work has featured in publications including *Opus* and *TRUE Africa*. Ruth is a Roundhouse Resident Artist and one of London's Boat Poets in Residence with Thames Festival Trust. Having performed across the UK and abroad, she has graced stages including Lagos International Poetry Festival and Hope College, USA.

Rebecca Tamás is a London based poet and lecturer, whose most recent pamphlet, *Savage*, came out with Clinic Press in 2017. Rebecca is the winner of the 2016 Manchester Poetry Prize, and has had work published in *The White Review, Poetry London, Poetry Review* and others. Her first collection, *WITCH*, will be published in 2019.

Joelle Taylor is an award-winning poet, playwright, essayist and author, and the founder of the Poetry Society's national youth slam championships. She has performed her poetry in venues ranging from the 100 Club to Parliament, and is the host for Out-Spoken poetry and music club in London. Her highly acclaimed new collection *Songs My Enemy Taught Me* was published in July 2017 by Out-Spoken Press.

Claire Trévien is the author of *The Shipwrecked House* (Penned in the Margins, 2013) and *Astéronymes* (Penned in the Margins, 2016). She founded Sabotage Reviews and runs its annual Saboteur Awards.

David Turner is the founding editor of the Lunar Poetry Podcasts series, has a City & Guilds certificate in Bench Joinery along with the accompanying scars, is known to the Southwark Community Mental Health Team as a 'service user' and has represented Norway in snow sculpting competitions. Originally from London but now living in Bristol. Widely unpublished. Working-class.

R.A. Villanueva's debut collection, *Reliquaria* (University of Nebraska Press) won the Prairie Schooner Book Prize. His work appears in *Poetry*, the *American Poetry Review*, *Guernica*, *Prac Crit*, *The Rialto*, and widely elsewhere. His honors include a commendation from the Forward Prizes, a Ninth Letter Literary Award, and fellowships from Kundiman, the Saltonstall Foundation for the Arts, and The Asian American Literary Review. A founding editor of *Tongue: A Journal of Writing & Art*, he lives in Brooklyn, NY.

Byron Vincent is one of BBC poetry season's New Talent Choices, and a regular at the UK's most prestigious literary and music festivals. His debut solo show, *Talk About Something You Like*, received much critical acclaim for its poignant and personal exploration of the mental health system. He's devised and presented several Radio 4 documentaries, exploring issues such as mental health, social housing, violence and ghettoization. Byron is a proud ambassador for mental health charity Rethink.

Pascal Vine is a two-time headlining performance poet from the Somerset levels. Pascal has multiple developmental disorders alongside chronic anxiety and OCD; their favoured coping method is spamming their Instagram with sonnets and other pithy offerings.

Antosh Wojcik is a poet, performer and lecturer at the University of Winchester. His cross-arts poetry and drumming show, *How To Keep Time: A Drum Solo for Dementia,* is produced by Penned In The Margins.

Reuben Woolley has been published in *Tears in the Fence, The Lighthouse Literary Journal, The Interpreter's House* and *Ink Sweat and Tears* among others. Published books: *the king is dead,* Oneiros, 2014; *dying notes,* Erbacce, 2015; *skins,* Hesterglock, 2016; *broken stories,* 20/20 Vision Media, 2017. His latest collection is *some time we are heroes,* The Corrupt Press, 2018. Runner-up: Overton Poetry Pamphlet competition and Erbacce Prize, 2015. Editor of the poetry webzines: *I am not a silent poet* and *The Curly Mind.*

Resources

Listed here are a few organisations, places and programmes that offer advice and support on a range of mental challenges. Of course, there are many more and we're unable to include them all, but we hope this, at least, provides a good place to start. Most of these services are free and confidential. Please use them when you need to.

Action on Postpartum Psychosis offers information and peer support to women experiencing postpartum psychosis. **www.app-network.org**

The Afiya Trust works to reduce inequalities in health and social care provision for people of colour. **www.nbta-uk.org.uk/partners/afiya-trust**

Aquarius is a West Midlands charity offering alcohol, drugs and gambling addiction recovery services and family support. **http://aquarius.org.uk**

Barnet Wellbeing Hub offers a person-centred approach, helping people in the borough to access local services. **www.barnetwellbeing.org.uk**

Beat is the UK's leading charity supporting anyone affected by eating disorders. **www.beateatingdisorders.org.uk**

Big White Wall is a safe and anonymous peer support community for people in any kind of emotional distress. **www.bigwhitewall.com**

BiPolar UK offers information, peer support and employment support to people affected by bipolar. **www.bipolaruk.org/**

Blurt Foundation offers helpful articles, a Mental Health Toolkit and self-care BuddyBoxes for people living with depression. **www.blurtitout.org**

CALM - the Campaign Against Living Miserably - is a charity dedicated to preventing male suicide. **www.thecalmzone.net**

CAMHS is the NHS's Child and Adolescent Mental Health Services, helping young people and their parents. Search for your area + 'camhs'.

Chinese Mental Health Association supports Chinese people in the UK suffering from mental health issues, and their carers. **www.cmha.org.uk**

Crisis teams are part of the NHS and provide urgent help if you're going through a mental health crisis. Search online for your area + 'crisis team'.

Drayton Park Women's Crisis House offers residential stays in a domestic setting, as an alternative to acute admission. **tinyurl.com/y8oeogjq**

Fegans is a Christian charity providing counselling for children, and parent support. **www.fegans.org.uk**

The Forward Trust (formerly RAPt and Blue Sky) runs programmes to help people with addiction break the cycle. **www.forwardtrust.org.uk**

Free Your Mind supports survivors of childhood domestic violence who experience mental illness as a result. **www.freeyourmindcic.com**

The Horse Course equine interventions help young people including those in care, PRU, prison or troubled families. **www.thehorsecourse.org**

Joseph Rowntree Foundation is a social change organisation whose work includes researching the links between austerity and mental health. **www.jrf.org.uk/people/mental-health**

Kids Inspire supports young people in Essex who are disadvantaged as a result of trauma or mental health issues. **https://kidsinspire.org.uk**

Lifeline Recovery Support Services helps individuals suffering from substance abuse disorders find long-term recovery. **www.lifelinerss.com**

Maytree is a charity offering people in suicidal crisis a free, safe place to stay, and befriending support. **www.maytree.org.uk**

Mental Health Foundation pioneers change to improve mental health, conducting research and influencing policy. **www.mentalhealth.org.uk**

The Mighty is an online community of over 1 million people, sharing stories and videos about their health challenges. **https://themighty.com**

Mind is a charity in England and Wales, helping people with mental ill health understand their rights and available treatment. **www.mind.org.uk**

Mind Over Matter runs spoken word and hip hop events dedicated to discussing mental health. **www.facebook.com/MindOverMatterLDN**

Mosaic Clubhouse assists mental health recovery for Lambeth residents, providing opportunities to work and learn. **www.mosaic-clubhouse.org**

My Time provides counselling and IAPT in community languages in the Midlands and the Isle of Wight. **www.recoveryfocus.org.uk/my-time**

NHS Recovery Centres exist in many boroughs across the UK, offering free and confidential support. Search for your area + 'recovery centre'.

No Panic specialises in self-help based recovery for people with anxiety. **www.nopanic.org.uk**

North Camden Recovery Team provides high quality care to people with psychotic illnesses. **https://tinyurl.com/yax9yvyv**

North Essex IAPT online portal connects adults in West, Mid and North East Essex to a range of talking therapies. **www.northessexiapt.nhs.uk**

Northumberland, Tyne & Wear NHS Foundation Trust has mental health, learning disabilities and neuro-rehabilitation services. **www.ntw.nhs.uk**

Psychologists for Social Change is a network of individuals applying psychology to policy and political action. **www.psychchange.org**

Recovery Focus is a national group of charities focused on aiding recovery from mental ill health and substance abuse. **www.recoveryfocus.org.uk**

Rethink Mental Illness campaigns to change policy and attitudes, offers advice and a national network of free support groups. **www.rethink.org**

Richmond Fellowship provides recovery-focused support and promotes social inclusion. **www.richmondfellowship.org.uk**

Samaritans offer a safe place to talk, day or night, whether you're suicidal or going through a tough time. Call 116 123 (UK) or 116 123 (ROI).

Studio Upstairs helps people transform their lives through creativity, and has branches in Bristol and London. **www.studioupstairs.org.uk**

The Tavistock and Portman Trust provides talking therapies for children, young people, adults and families. **https://tavistockandportman.nhs.uk**

Time to Change work with communities, schools, workplaces and the media to end mental health discrimination. **www.time-to-change.org.uk**

Woman's Trust provides women-only support services to help deal with the effects of domestic violence and abuse. **www.womanstrust.org.uk**

Young Minds campaigns for better mental health support for children and young people. **https://youngminds.org.uk**

Other titles by Bad Betty Press

Solomon's World
Jake Wild Hall

Unremember
Joel Auterson

In My Arms
Setareh Ebrahimi

The Story Is
Kate B Hall

Forthcoming in 2018

BAD BETTY SHOTS:

I'm Shocked	Iris Colomb
Ode to Laura Smith	Aischa Daughtery
The Pale Fox	Katie Metcalfe
TIGER	Rebecca Tamás

Death of a Clown
Tom Bland

Lightning Source UK Ltd.
Milton Keynes UK
UKHW01f2153100818
327017UK00010B/151/P

9 781999 714741